Taking Charge in Your New Leadership Role

A step-by-step guide to preparing for any new leadership position

Michael Watkins
Harvard Business School

Copyright ©2001 by Harvard Business School Publishing. All rights reserved. No part of this publication may be reproduced, stored in a retrieval system, used in a spreadsheet, or transmitted in any form or by any means – electronic, mechanical, photocopying, recording, or otherwise – without prior written permission of the publisher. Printed in the United States of America.

CONTENTS

Copyright ©2001 by Harvard Business School Publishing. All rights reserved.

ACKNOWLEDGMENTS

Many people contributed to the creation of this workbook. Foremost is my *Right from the Start* co-author Dan Ciampa, who got me interested in leadership transitions in the first place. His deep understanding of the challenges that managers face in taking on new senior-level positions continues to inform my thinking. Dan is a gifted counselor of leaders and a good friend.

This project grew out of work I did to develop Transition Leadership programs in conjunction with Johnson & Johnson. Inaki Bastarrika of J&J's Management Education and Development (MED) Department convinced me to work with this excellent company, initiating a rewarding research partnership. Ron Bossert, a Director of MED, was instrumental in conceiving of and overseeing the development of the J&J Transition Leadership Forum and the Business Leaders' Program. Ron also introduced me to leading line managers whose experience contributed greatly to the development of these programs, including Bill Dearstyne, Colleen Goggins, Dennis Longstreet, Peter Tattle, and Tony Vernon. Senior HR practitioners, including Paul Culleton, Diane Seddon, Steve Ganzler, Mike Thomas, and Vikki Walker, also provided invaluable guidance.

Thanks also to Colleen Olson, Steve Cohen, and Andrea Deege of Dove Consulting and to Ron Meeks of Executive Development Associates for their professionalism in supporting development of the J&J Transition Leadership Forum and Business Leaders' Program.

Some key transition leadership concepts presented in this workbook were developed by others, notably John Gabarro on waves of change, Noel Tichy on technical, cultural, and political dimensions of organizations, David Lax and Jim Sebenius on sequencing in coalition building, and Ron Heifetz on work avoidance. Thanks to them for their insights.

Finally, many thanks to my editor Ann Goodsell for her support and efforts to make this workbook more accessible.

Copyright ©2001 by Harvard Business School Publishing. All rights reserved.

A NOTE FROM THE PUBLISHER

Many users of *Taking Charge in Your New Leadership Role* are individual managers striving to improve their self-understanding and skills. However, this workbook is also ideal for use by groups of managers undergoing training together. Note, for example, that we have perforated the pages and inserted blank pages to facilitate removal of completed exercises, which can be submitted to a group discussion leader.

To order additional copies call (800) 545-7685 or (617) 783-7600. You can also send inquiries by e-mail: custserv@hbsp.harvard.edu.

If you are considering the purchase of workbooks for a large group, be sure to inquire about quantity discounts.

Harvard Business School Publishing has many other materials on the topic of leadership. Here are just a few recent examples:

* *Right from the Start: Taking Charge in a New Leadership Role* (Ciampa and Watkins), an HBS Press book co-written by the author of this workbook. Product no. 7501.

* *Level 5 Leadership: The Triumph of Humility and Fierce Resolve*, a Harvard Business Review OnPoint Enhanced Edition reprint. Product no. 5831.

* *GE's Two-Decade Transformation: Jack Welch's Leadership*, a multimedia case study. Product no. 301040

* *Executive-Team Leadership*, a reprint from The Balanced Scorecard Report. Product no. b0009a.

To examine the full range of our materials on leadership, visit our Web site at www.hbsp.harvard.edu.

INTRODUCTION: THE CHALLENGE

Congratulations! If you are reading this workbook, you are probably transitioning into a new leadership role. If so, you are in good company. Every year thousands of managers—more than 600,000 annually in Fortune 500 companies alone—transition into new jobs. The typical CEO of a Fortune 100 company has made seven major transitions—moves between functions, business units, or companies— by the time he or she reaches the top. But for every successful CEO, there are many talented managers who stumble along the way, damaging their careers and the organizations they were charged to lead. You've picked up this book because you don't want to be one of them.

Why do you need to plan your transition?

Your actions during the first few months in your new job will have a disproportionate impact on your ultimate success or failure. Transitions are pivotal, in part because everyone in your new organization is expecting change to occur. But because you don't know the organization and haven't developed solid working relationships or personal support systems, they are also periods of great vulnerability. Your new boss, your subordinates, other employees, and key external stakeholders are all forming early impressions that will powerfully shape their expectations and actions, either enlarging or restricting your scope for action. If you build momentum during the transition, it will continue to propel you throughout your tenure in your new job. If you get caught in vicious cycles, it will be hard to claw your way back.

What are the imperatives of a successful transition?

Transitioning into a new job poses a demanding set of imperatives for the new leader:

- ❏ *Acquiring knowledge quickly.* Even the best-prepared new leaders don't know all they need to know in order to function effectively in a new organization. So you have to systematically plan to learn about your new organization and its technologies, markets, culture, and politics.

- ❏ *Establishing new working relationships.* Having left behind well-established working relationships with your former boss, subordinates, peers, and support staff, you must work rapidly to establish productive new relationships. And you have to do this while you struggle to get your arms around the organization.

- ❏ *Juggling organizational and personal transitions*. While you are striving to get up to speed with your new organization, you may have to manage wrenching personal and family transitions.

- ❏ *Managing expectations*. Expectations of new leaders are understandably high, which creates risks. The process of managing expectations begins as early as possible, even while you are still being considered for the new position.

- ❏ *Maintaining personal equilibrium.* Transitions place extreme physical and emotional demands on new leaders. You will need to find ways to conserve your energy and preserve your emotional balance and perspective—to stay on "the rested edge."

To meet these challenges, it helps to have a framework for planning and prioritizing your actions. This workbook provides it. It will help you identify potential pitfalls and diagnose the unique challenges of your new situation. Then it will provide a proven model for planning your time, both before entry and during your first few months in your new job.

Copyright ©2001 by Harvard Business School Publishing. All rights reserved.

Meeting the challenge: Seven rules

As you transition into your new leadership role, seven rules can provide a framework for orienting yourself and setting goals.

Rule 1: Leverage the time before entry.

Use the time between selection and formal entry to jump-start the transition process. This pre-entry period represents precious uninterrupted time to assess the organization and formulate ideas about what needs to be done. Before setting foot in your new office, learn as much as possible about your organization's strategy, strengths, and weaknesses and develop some hypotheses to begin testing.

Rule 2: Organize to learn.

Entering a new organization can be like sailing in a dense fog. Coping with limited visibility, you must exercise caution while you get your bearings. Because expectations are high and time is precious, you must organize to learn as rapidly as possible about the organization, especially about its culture and politics.

Rule 3: Secure early wins.

It is crucial for employees to perceive that momentum is building during the transition. Within six months, you must have noticeably energized people and focused them on the organization's most pressing problems, using techniques that have immediate and dramatic impact. Early wins are a powerful way to get people pumped up.

Rule 4: Lay a foundation for major improvements.

Early wins can help you get off to a good start, but they are not sufficient for continued success. To meet your boss's and your own expectations, you must also lay a foundation for the deeper cultural changes needed to sustain improvement in the organization's performance. The process is like launching a two-stage rocket into orbit; early wins lift you off the ground, and foundation-building provides the thrust necessary to avoid falling back to earth.

Rule 5: Build winning coalitions.

However much you learn and plan, you can achieve little alone. Powerful individuals and groups inside and outside the organization must perceive it as in their interests to help you realize your goals, and they must act accordingly. Building supportive coalitions and either reorienting or weakening unsupportive existing coalitions alters the power structure to favor implementation of change initiatives.

Rule 6: Create a personal vision of the organization's future.

Whether or not visioning comes naturally to you, you have to engage in imaginative visualization in order to know where you want to take the organization. More encompassing and unified than goals, a personal vision of the organization as it could be can organize your thoughts and observations and can eventually evolve into a shared vision.

Rule 7: Manage yourself.

Given the amount you need to learn about new products, markets, and the organization, a clear head is a must. Above all, you must find ways to maintain perspective and avoid isolation. Self-diagnosis and reflection are important tools for achieving these goals. You can gain additional perspective by soliciting appropriate advice and counsel.

HOW TO USE THIS WORKBOOK

This workbook offers step-by-step guidance for taking charge in a new leadership role. Part One focuses on fundamentals: common traps into which unwary new leaders fall, types of transitional situations, and a model for planning to take charge. Part Two digs into four key transition leadership challenges, providing guidance on how to accelerate your learning process, influence key people, align your organization, and manage yourself in a stressful situation. Part Three outlines a step-by-step planning process, in the course of which you will identify long-term goals, develop a personal vision, figure out where and how to achieve some crucially important early wins, and lay a foundation for longer-term success. Part Four contains assessment instruments that you can use to evaluate your style and resources.

> *You should begin by scanning the entire workbook. Look in particular at Part Three on Building Momentum, beginning on page 117. This is the culmination of all the work you will do in Parts One and Two, so it's important to take the time to understand where you will end up.*

As you proceed through the workbook, you will be asked to answer questions for which you will not have definitive answers. Answer them as best you can, recognizing that your knowledge and understanding will inevitably be partial during your first few months in a new position.

This workbook also calls for some hardheaded self-scrutiny—not psycho-analyzing, but recognizing your own patterns and preferences, strengths and shortcomings. Before reading further, set aside roughly an hour (not necessarily in a single sitting) to fill out the Personal Assessment Inventories in Part Four (see page 153). The workbook will draw on these self-assessments repeatedly, so it's essential to fill them out now. Resist the urge to complete the assessments hastily or on autopilot. Thorough responses will pay off in better planning.

> *You will get substantially more out of the self-assessments in this workbook if you also get others to assess you. As soon as possible you should make copies of the observer assessment instruments in Part Five (see page 171), choose the recipients, and distribute them right away. Ask people you trust—family, friends, former bosses, and former subordinates—to fill them out and return them to you, within a few days if possible. You should not open them until you have filled out the assessments yourself. You also should wait until you have all of them in hand and they can be read together. Resist the temptation to peek as it will diminish their value.*

Copyright ©2001 by Harvard Business School Publishing. All rights reserved.

THIS PAGE INTENTIONALLY LEFT BLANK

PART ONE:
FUNDAMENTALS OF EFFECTIVE
TRANSITION MANAGEMENT

Leaders who fail to make successful transitions tend to stumble into classic traps and get derailed in predictable ways. All transitions are not created equal, so it's essential to understand the particular challenges posed by startups, turnarounds, and realignments, and your own strengths and weaknesses in each of these situations. You also need to understand how your transition fits within the longer-term era of change that you will undertake in your new organization. Your transition should both help you build momentum and lay the foundation for longer-term success.

Once you understand your situation fully, you will be ready to plan to take charge, which involves defining your goals and organizing to learn, to influence, and to redesign the organization. At an even more fundamental level, you have to manage yourself during the first few complicated, ambiguous, and exhausting months on the job.

Copyright ©2001 by Harvard Business School Publishing. All rights reserved.

AVOIDING COMMON TRAPS

Given all you need to do, and the stresses of taking charge in a new leadership role, you will be at risk of succumbing to certain common pitfalls. To avoid derailment, keep the following traps squarely in mind:

Trap	Description	Results
Falling behind the learning curve	Before beginning your new job, you devote most of your time to wrapping up your previous responsibilities or taking time off.	You don't learn what you need to know to make sound early decisions, leading to judgments that damage your credibility.
Becoming isolated	You spend too much time reading financial and operating reports and not enough time talking with employees and other key constituencies.	You don't build the relationships and information conduits necessary to understand what is really going on.
Coming in with the answer	You come in with your mind made up about the problem and the solution.	Narrow fixes for complex problems alienate people and squander opportunities for good solutions.
Sticking with the existing team too long	You retain subordinates with a record of mediocre performance in the belief that your leadership will make a difference.	You waste precious time and energy trying to compensate for the team's weaknesses.
Attempting to do too much	You rush off in all directions, launching multiple initiatives in the hope that some will pay off.	People become confused, and a critical mass of resources never gets focused on key initiatives.
Allowing yourself to be captured by the wrong people	You create the perception that you listen to some people and not others.	Your information is inadequate, and potential supporters are alienated; your decisions are based on poor advice.
Setting unrealistic expectations	You don't negotiate your initial mandate and establish clear, achievable objectives.	You may perform well but still fail to meet your boss's expectations.

Your overriding goal: Build momentum

Each of these traps enmeshes its victims in a *vicious cycle*. By failing to learn enough at the outset, for example, you can make bad initial decisions that damage your credibility. Then, because people don't trust your judgment, it can become still more difficult to learn what you need to know. More and more energy gets consumed compensating for miscalculations.

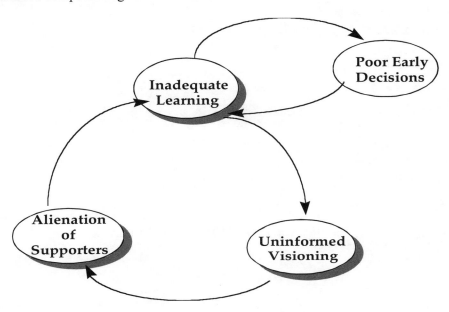

Your overarching goal during the transition is not just to avoid vicious cycles; you need to create *virtuous cycles* that help you to build momentum. Good initial decisions founded on effective learning, for example, bolster your personal credibility. As people come to trust your judgment, your ability to learn accelerates and you equip yourself to make sound calls on tougher issues.

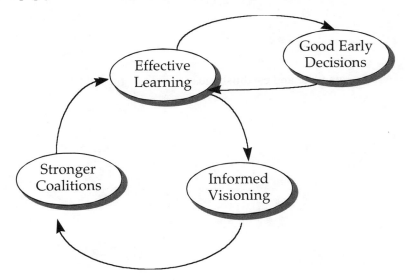

Copyright ©2001 by Harvard Business School Publishing. All rights reserved.

THIS PAGE INTENTIONALLY LEFT BLANK

Assessing your vulnerability to pitfalls

Reflect on your past transitions into new leadership roles. On a scale of 1-5, how susceptible have you been to each of the classic traps? Rate each separately.

Trap	Your susceptibility
Falling behind the learning curve	1----------2----------3----------4----------5 low high
Becoming isolated	1----------2----------3----------4----------5 low high
Coming in with the answer	1----------2----------3----------4----------5 low high
Sticking with the existing team too long	1----------2----------3----------4----------5 low high
Attempting to do too much	1----------2----------3----------4----------5 low high
Allowing yourself to be captured by the wrong people	1----------2----------3----------4----------5 low high
Setting unrealistic expectations	1----------2----------3----------4----------5 low high

Now look at page 173 in each of the Observer Assessments of Transition Experience that you distributed to trusted people and compare yours to theirs. Are you surprised by any of their responses? If their assessments differ from yours, why do you think that is the case?

_____

_____

_____

_____

_____

_____

Copyright ©2001 by Harvard Business School Publishing. All rights reserved.

What makes you susceptible?

Focus on the trap to which you assigned the highest ranking. What do you think makes you particularly susceptible to this trap? What is it about your style or experience that leaves you vulnerable?

_____

_____

_____

_____

_____

Now look at your trusted advisors' answers to the same questions in the Observer Assessments (see page 174). If their answers are different from yours, why do you think that is the case? Do your advisors all point to the same issues? If not, why do you think they see things differently?

_____

_____

_____

_____

Avoiding vicious cycles

Given your own answers and those of your advisors, what actions can you take to avoid creating vicious cycles early in your transition? List three specific actions. Force yourself to think of three actions even if one approach dominates your thoughts.

❑ _____

❑ _____

❑ _____

DIAGNOSING YOUR SITUATION

Four classic types of situations that new leaders encounter are *startup, turnaround, realignment,* and *sustaining success*. As summarized below, different types of transition situations pose specific and dissimilar challenges. Each also provides unique resources upon which you can draw.

Type	Description	Challenges	Resources
Startup	Assembling the capabilities (people, financing, technology) to get a new business or project off the ground.	❑ Building structures and systems from scratch without a clear framework or boundaries. ❑ Welding together a cohesive high-performing team. ❑ Making do with limited resources.	❑ You can do things right from the beginning. ❑ People are energized by the possibilities. ❑ There is no preexisting rigidity in people's thinking.
Turnaround	Turning around a business acknowledged to be in serious trouble.	❑ Re-energizing demoralized employees and other stakeholders. ❑ Handling time pressure and having a quick and decisive impact. ❑ Going deep enough with painful cuts and difficult personnel choices.	❑ Everyone recognizes change is necessary. ❑ Affected constituencies offer significant external support. ❑ A little success goes a long way. ❑ You have some credibility at the outset.
Realignment	Changing the culture of a previously successful organization that now faces serious challenges.	❑ Convincing employees that change is necessary. ❑ Restructuring the top team and refocusing the organization.	❑ The organization has significant pockets of strength. ❑ People want to see themselves as successful.
Sustaining success	Succeeding a highly-regarded leader in a business with a stellar record of accomplishment.	❑ Living in the shadow of a revered leader and dealing with the team he or she created. ❑ Playing good defense by avoiding decisions that cause problems. ❑ Finding ways to take the business to the next level.	❑ A strong team may already be in place. ❑ People are motivated to succeed. ❑ Foundations for continued success (such as the product pipeline) may be in place.

Whether you are taking over an entire organization or leading a unit or initiative within your existing organization, you can use this framework to assess your strengths and weaknesses. A startup, for example, may be a new entrepreneurial venture or the launch of a new product in an established company. Likewise, a turnaround can involve a new (to you) business or a troubled unit within your company.

Copyright ©2001 by Harvard Business School Publishing. All rights reserved.

THIS PAGE INTENTIONALLY LEFT BLANK

Assessing your preferences

Different transition situations demand different skills. Someone who is good at turnarounds may be ineffective in realignment situations that call for painstaking work to develop coalitions in support of change. Likewise, someone who is good at realignments may not move quickly and decisively enough for a turnaround situation.

Which of the four types of situations – startup, turnaround, realignment, sustaining success – do you most prefer? Why?

_____

_____

_____

Which do you least prefer? Why?

_____

_____

_____

What do these preferences say about your strengths and weaknesses as a transition leader?

_____

_____

_____

_____

_____

_____

Copyright ©2001 by Harvard Business School Publishing. All rights reserved.

The development grid

The development grid is a tool for charting your professional history and development. The *rows of the grid are key functions* in which you might have worked – marketing, sales, operations, and so on. The *columns are the types of business situations* that you have been a part of – startup, turnaround, realignment, and sustaining success.

You should use the grid to chart <u>each</u> management position you have occupied so far in your career, as well as any major project-related assignments in which you have participated. For example, suppose your first professional job was in marketing in an organization (or unit within a larger organization) that was in the midst of a turnaround. If so, you would place a circle with a "1" in it (indicating your first management position) in that cell of the matrix.

Your next position may have been in sales in a new unit (for dealing with a new product or project) – which is a startup situation. So you should put a circle with a "2" in it in that cell. At the same time you may have been part of a task force dealing with operations issues in the startup. So you should put a triangle (indicating major project assignment) with a "2" in it (indicating it was part of your second significant professional position) in the appropriate cell.

Do this for all the managerial jobs you have held so far. Then connect the dots in order to illuminate your professional trajectory. Are there columns or rows that are blank? What are the implications for your readiness for general management positions? For your potential blind spots?

	Startup	Turnaround	Realignment	Sustaining Success
Marketing				
Sales				
Finance				
HR				
Operations				
Information Management				
R&D				

 = full-time position

 = short-term assignment

Assessing your situational vulnerabilities

Which of the four types of situations are you entering this time?

_____

_____

What are the three most demanding challenges you expect to face?

1. _____
2. _____
3. _____

Think about your skills and status. What are your particular vulnerabilities in this situation? *Note that your status in the organization can create vulnerabilities. For example, people brought in from outside often have trouble in realignment and success-sustaining situations; it's much easier for them to lead startups or turnarounds.*

_____

_____

_____

_____

_____

What implications do you see for the kinds of support you will need?

_____

_____

_____

_____

Copyright ©2001 by Harvard Business School Publishing. All rights reserved.

THIS PAGE INTENTIONALLY LEFT BLANK

PLANNING FOR A NEW ERA

This transition is undoubtedly one in a series of professional challenges you have undertaken over the course of your career. If you are like most managers, you have spent two to four years in each of your previous positions. Unless you are at the very top of an organization—the average CEO has a tenure of seven years—you will probably spend roughly the same amount of time in your new position. You can think of this two- to three-year period as your *era* in the organization. If all goes well, you will make your transition, progressively gain mastery, accomplish your goals, and eventually leave to begin a new era in a new organization.

Clearly, you should plan your transition in light of what you intend to accomplish by the end of your two- to three-year era. What are your era goals and what are the implications for what you need to do during your transition?

So as you undertake your transition, you should begin to spell out your long-term "A-item priorities" for the business—and for your own personal development—early on. In some cases your priorities will be evident at the start (perhaps because they are clearly specified by your boss); in other situations it may take a while for you to gain the necessary insight. It's a mistake to impose a rigid deadline on yourself for committing to A-item priorities. But if you let it slide too long, your efforts are likely to remain unfocused.

Establishing A-item priorities is about figuring out where you want to end up and then managing with those ends in mind. We will look at the process of establishing A-item priorities in Part Three. If you do a good job of defining your long-term priorities, you will be equipped to continually assess the effectiveness of what you are doing in the short term

Use the space below to assess your last two or three years in your <u>previous organization</u>. To what extent did you achieve your A-item priorities? If you didn't do so to your own satisfaction, why was that the case?

Copyright ©2001 by Harvard Business School Publishing. All rights reserved.

THIS PAGE INTENTIONALLY LEFT BLANK

Preparing to implement waves of change

The *pacing* of the changes you implement will not be steady. Effective new leaders introduce change in waves, not at an even pace. As illustrated below, you should therefore plan for an era consisting of four distinct stages. The times given are averages. The amount of change you implement should vary depending on your situation.

Stage 1. Entry: lasts up to six months, beginning when you enter the job and ending when you initiate the first major wave of changes.

Stage 2. Immersion: lasts five to eleven months, during which you continue to implement the first wave of changes, observe their impact, learn more deeply, and plan the next wave of (usually more drastic) changes.

Stage 3. Reshaping: lasts three to six months, devoted to the second major wave of change.

Stage 4. Consolidation: lasts six or more months, during which you observe the outcome of the second wave and make the necessary adjustments in a third, less extreme wave of change.

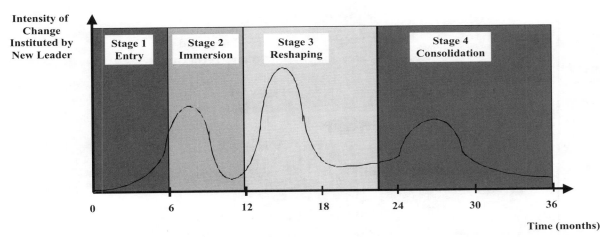

What are implications of planning to implement waves of change? First, you should plan to devote enough time to consolidating each major set of changes, observing, learning, and preparing for the next wave. Trying to maintain continuous change is a sure recipe for overwhelming the organization.

Second, be careful to match the intensity of the changes you implement to the organization's capacity to absorb them. Pushing too little change in each wave is a lost opportunity; pushing too much will result in fatigue and poor execution. Your goal is to keep the pot at a steady simmer, not to let it cool down or boil over.

Third, pay attention to the timing and coherence of the changes you implement in each wave. Your primary focus in the first wave should be on early wins. The second wave should focus on deeper changes that will lead to sustainable breakthrough improvements in performance.

Fourth and critically, *recognize that the actual pattern will vary depending on the type of situation you are in.* A turnaround, for example, will require more and deeper change early, while realignments require substantially more preparation.

19

Copyright ©2001 by Harvard Business School Publishing. All rights reserved.

THE TAKING-CHARGE MODEL

By now it should be obvious that you need to plan your transition in order to be successful. Disciplined use of the taking-charge model illustrated below can help guide your actions. The top half of the pyramid identifies the key goals you will need to achieve during your transition: defining your long-term *A-item priorities*, securing *early wins,* and *laying a foundation* for deeper change. The bottom half highlights four fundamental challenges you will have to surmount: the *learning challenge*, the *influence challenge*, the *design challenge*, and the *self-management challenge.*

Defining your goals

Your overarching goal during your transition will be to build momentum toward *achieving your A-item priorities.* A-items are the key business objectives you need to reach within two to three years in order to meet your boss's (and your own) expectations. To build momentum during your transition, you have to *secure early wins* while also *laying a foundation* for deeper change. Approaches to doing so will be described in detail in Part Three.

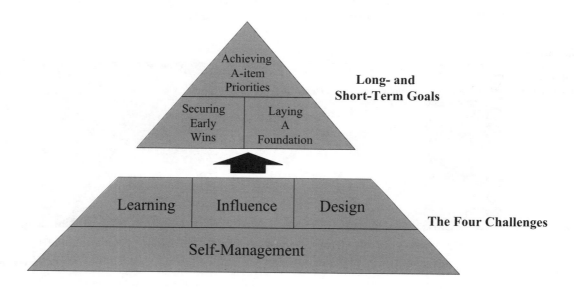

Meeting the four challenges

Securing early wins and laying a foundation for change depends on your ability to meet four fundamental challenges during your transition:

❑ **The learning challenge:** Learning about your new organization fast, before entry and during your first few months on the job.

❑ **The influence challenge:** Building personal credibility and productive working relationships with your new boss, subordinates, employees, and key external stakeholders.

❑ **The design challenge:** Aligning the organization's strategy, structure, systems, skills, and culture.

❑ **The self-management challenge:** Maintaining perspective and emotional balance while dealing with the pressures of a new position.

Approaches to meeting these challenges are explored in detail in the next part.

The transition timeline

For our purposes, the transition period begins when you learn that you are being considered for the job, and ends six months after you begin it. This period has three main phases:

- ❑ *Pre-selection*: from learning that you are being considered until learning that you've got the job
- ❑ *The fuzzy front end:* from selection until formal entry
- ❑ *Taking charge*: from entry until the end of your first six months on the job

The front end is fuzzy because the period between selection and formal entry can range from days to weeks. Furthermore, you don't yet have any authority, or much access to information. This is nevertheless a crucial time for learning about your new organization. It's also time that can be squandered on wrapping up your responsibilities in your former job.

The taking-charge phase is demarcated by certain key milestones: you should aim to fulfill important visible goals by the end of the first day, first week, first month, and first three months.

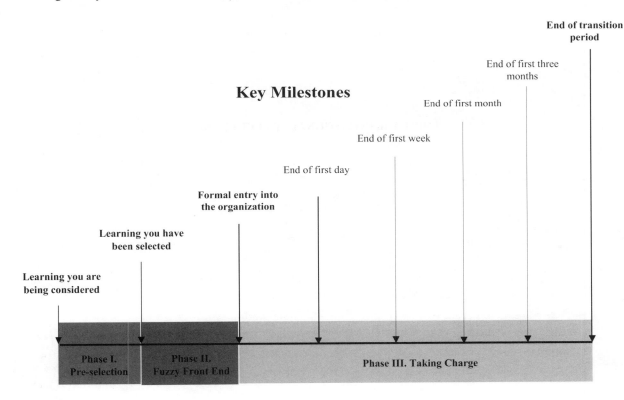

Copyright ©2001 by Harvard Business School Publishing. All rights reserved.

THIS PAGE INTENTIONALLY LEFT BLANK

PART TWO:
THE FOUR CHALLENGES OF TRANSITION

Building your transition from the bottom up calls for thinking carefully about how you will approach four tasks: learning, influence, design, and self-management. Part Two will lead you through each of these challenges. By the end of Part Two, you will be ready to answer the following key questions:

❑ *Learning:* What do I need to learn most urgently, and how can I accelerate my learning?

❑ *Influence:* Who are the individuals critical to my success, and how can I build credibility with them?

❑ *Design:* How should I pursue alignment between my team and the strategy, structure, systems, skills, and culture of the organization?

❑ *Self-management:* What are my characteristic personal shortcomings during transitions and how can I compensate for them?

Copyright ©2001 by Harvard Business School Publishing. All rights reserved.

THE LEARNING CHALLENGE

Taking in information during your first days in a new job is like drinking from a firehose: there is far too much to be absorbed about strategies, products, markets, technologies, and systems, not to mention people. It's difficult to know what to pay attention to. Far more than any other phase of a job, transitions demand efficiency and effectiveness in learning.

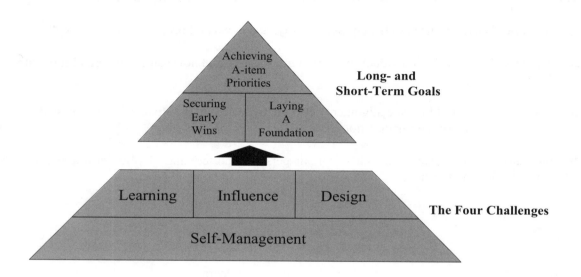

Principles for effective learning

Three basic principles can help you figure out what you need to learn:

You don't have to learn everything right away. You can't hope to understand your organization's sources of innovation or political pecking order in your first week on the job. The good news is that you don't need to, because you have some time before you must make big decisions. You only need to learn enough to make sure that your early decisions are good ones.

You should learn with a point of view. Learning that is disciplined and shaped by a point of view is far more effective than random information-gathering even if the point of view ultimately turns out to need refinement. Begin to develop your point of view—your assessment of key problems and opportunities—prior to entry, along with specific hypotheses to test once you are in the chair.

It gets harder to learn as time passes. When you first arrive, you are relatively "pure": living in the organization hasn't yet affected the way you see the world. Though your outsider status represents a vulnerability, you can see things through relatively objective eyes. You don't have a stake in what has gone before. The more time you spend in the organization, the more your objectivity will be clouded. Becoming "of" the organization is a good thing, but it comes at a cost: clear-headed learning gets harder.

Undertaking technical, cultural, and political learning

Transitions call for three distinct types of learning:

- ❑ **Technical learning:** Mastering (1) the nature and key features of products and target markets and customers, (2) current strategy and its organizational requirements, and (3) the organization's technological and human capabilities.

- ❑ **Cultural learning:** Identifying your organization's cultural strengths and weaknesses, norms and values, accepted ways of working, and habits that have contributed to its unique character.

- ❑ **Political learning:** Assessing how decisions are made; singling out who to consult; identifying the most influential coalitions and those most likely to support the changes you envision.

The hardest realities to master are organizational culture and politics. There is no report to read or objective data to analyze. You can learn about both only from people who work in or interact with the organization. But people are often uncommunicative about politics and oblivious to the culture. Both are terribly important: failure to understand culture and politics almost always brings about derailment. So you must observe carefully, look for patterns, develop theories, and evaluate evidence systematically.

Use the space below to assess your strengths and weaknesses in learning in each of these three domains:

_____

_____

_____

_____

_____

_____

_____

_____

_____

_____

Copyright ©2001 by Harvard Business School Publishing. All rights reserved.

Establishing learning priorities

Specific learning targets tailored to your unique circumstances will keep you focused during transition. Use the tables below to think through your learning priorities for the period prior to entry and for your first week on the job.

Learning prior to entry

Reread the definitions of technical, cultural, and political learning above, and identify some pre-entry priorities for each. If you are already on the job, identify what you would like to have learned before entry if you had it to do over.

Type	Description	Priorities for learning before entry
Technical	Markets, products, technologies, and processes	
Cultural	Norms and values	
Political	Sources of power, coalitions, and networks of influence	

Learning during the first week

Now define technical, cultural, and political learning priorities for your first week on the job. If the first week is already behind you, pinpoint what you would like to have learned.

Type	Description	Priorities for learning during the first week
Technical	Markets, products, technologies, and processes	
Cultural	Norms and values	
Political	Sources of power, coalitions, and networks of influence	

Now take a look at the Guidelines for Establishing Learning Goals for the time before entry and first week on the job (see pages 184 and 185). How do your goals differ from those that are outlined? What do you think accounts for the differences?

Understanding your learning style

Like it or not, you have a *learning style*: a set of preferences about what and how you like to learn. The corollary is that you will have both strengths and potential blind spots in self-directed learning. It's essential to recognize the latter and work to compensate for them.

Assessing what you like to learn

Start by looking at your assessment of your problem preferences in the Assessment of Leadership Style (see pages 161 and 162). This assessment pinpoints the *business functions* you gravitate toward and your preferences with regard to *technical, cultural*, and *political* problems. Do you tend to give short shrift to certain business functions? If so, how will you avoid being blindsided by problems in those areas? Are you uneasy about your instincts in the cultural or political realm? Many gifted leaders prefer concrete technical issues to culture and politics. For others, technical learning is a weak point.

Based on these assessments, what do you least like to learn about?

_____

_____

_____

_____

Assessing how you like to learn

Now look at your responses in the Assessment of Leadership Style about your learning style (see page 164). This assessment zeroes in on *how* you learn best. On balance, do you prefer to learn from hard data or soft data? What does this preference signify for what you see and don't see? Are you experiential in your approach to learning—preferring to dive in and try to figure things out —or more conceptual in orientation? How does this inclination influence your ability to learn during a transition?

What are the implications for your vulnerabilities?

_____

_____

_____

_____

Copyright ©2001 by Harvard Business School Publishing. All rights reserved.

THIS PAGE INTENTIONALLY LEFT BLANK

Identifying whom to learn from

Identifying the most promising sources of insight into the organization will make your learning more efficient and effective. Key sources of knowledge are summarized in the diagram below. Builders are the people who manufacture your products or deliver your services. Integrators are people who coordinate or facilitate cross-functional interaction.

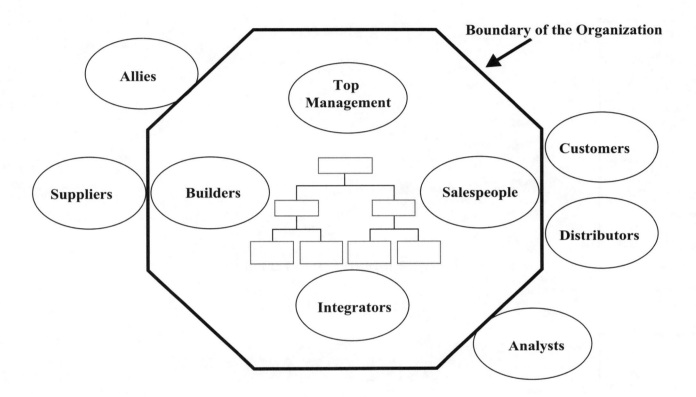

Observing from multiple points of view

To help structure your learning, think in terms of examining your new organization from five distinct points of view:

- ❏ from the outside in
- ❏ from the inside out
- ❏ from the bottom up
- ❏ from the top down
- ❏ from the middle sideways

Copyright ©2001 by Harvard Business School Publishing. All rights reserved.

THIS PAGE INTENTIONALLY LEFT BLANK

Looking in from outside

Looking from the outside in calls for consulting with customers, suppliers, distributors, and others who interact with your organization. Talk to knowledgeable representatives of the key external groups listed below. How does each perceive your organization? What do they see as its strengths? Its weaknesses? If you are heading up a unit within a larger entity, it may be appropriate to consult internal suppliers and customers.

Group	Perceptions of your organization's strengths	Perceptions of your organization's weaknesses
Customers		
Suppliers		
Distributors		
Strategic allies		
Analysts		
Local community and government leaders		

What are the implications of your outside-in observations for the key challenges you face?

_____

_____

_____

_____

Copyright ©2001 by Harvard Business School Publishing. All rights reserved.

THIS PAGE INTENTIONALLY LEFT BLANK

Looking out from inside

Looking from the inside out calls for consulting knowledgeable people on the front lines of your organization who deal with customers, suppliers, distributors, and other external stakeholders. Doing so equips you to look at your organization's key interfaces from both sides. Consult with representatives of the internal groups listed below. How does each perceive your organization, and especially its dealings with key external constituencies? What do they see as its strengths? Its weaknesses? What problems do they mention that others in the organization don't? Do their impressions match what your external informants told you? If not, what do you think accounts for the discrepancy?

Group	Perceptions of your organization's strengths	Perceptions of your organization's weaknesses
Salespeople		
New product/service developers		
Purchasing		
Logistics and distribution		
Quality		
Corporate affairs and investor relations		

What are the implications of your inside-out observations for the key challenges you face?

_____

_____

_____

_____

Copyright ©2001 by Harvard Business School Publishing. All rights reserved.

THIS PAGE INTENTIONALLY LEFT BLANK

Looking up from the bottom

For the view from the bottom up, look to knowledgeable first-level people in key functions. Consult representatives of each of the internal groups listed below. How does each perceive your organization? What do they see as its strengths? Its weaknesses? What problems do they report that others in the organization don't? Their perspective will tell you how people further down in the organizational hierarchy perceive what is going on higher up.

Group	Perceptions of your organization's strengths	Perceptions of your organization's weaknesses
Production/service workers and supervisors		
Research and development		
Marketing		
Finance		
Information technology		

What are the implications of your bottom-up observations for the key challenges you face?

_____

_____

_____

_____

Copyright ©2001 by Harvard Business School Publishing. All rights reserved.

THIS PAGE INTENTIONALLY LEFT BLANK

Looking down from the top

Looking from the top down calls for consulting senior managers in the units listed below. How does each perceive your organization? What do they see as its strengths? Its weaknesses? What problems do they observe that others in the organization don't? Do their impressions match those of people lower down in the organization? If not, why not? Is there consistency between what the top people tell you and what their direct reports say?

Group	Perceptions of your organization's strengths	Perceptions of your organization's weaknesses
Operations		
Research and development		
Marketing		
Finance		
Information technology		

What are the implications of your top-down observations for the key challenges you face?

_____

_____

_____

_____

Copyright ©2001 by Harvard Business School Publishing. All rights reserved.

THIS PAGE INTENTIONALLY LEFT BLANK

Looking sideways from the middle

Integrators—people who sit at key cross-functional interfaces—are in a position to look laterally from a central vantage point. Consult with the kinds of people listed below. How does each perceive your organization? What do they see as its strengths? Its weaknesses? What problems do they discern that others in the organization don't? Do their impressions match what people in the functions say? If not, why not?

Group	Perceptions of your organization's strengths	Perceptions of your organization's weaknesses
Product managers		
Project and program leaders		
Heads of task forces and working groups		
Informal liaisons between functional groups		

What are the implications of your lateral observations for the key challenges you face?

_____

_____

_____

_____

Copyright ©2001 by Harvard Business School Publishing. All rights reserved.

THIS PAGE INTENTIONALLY LEFT BLANK

Using structured methods to accelerate your learning

Having roughed out what you need to learn during your transition and identified promising sources of knowledge, the next task is to figure out *how* to learn more efficiently and effectively. Of course, plenty of learning takes place opportunistically during unstructured encounters like meetings. But structured approaches such as those outlined below can accelerate the pace.

Method	Uses
Organizational-climate and employee-satisfaction surveys	Yields information about culture and morale. Many organizations do such surveys regularly, and a database may already be available. If not, consider inaugurating a regular survey of employee perceptions.
Structured sets of interviews of slices of the organization	A quick way to identify shared and divergent perceptions of opportunities and problems. Horizontal slices interview people at the same level in different departments; vertical slices bore down through multiple levels. Whichever dimension you choose, ask the same questions and look for similarities and differences in people's responses.
Focus groups	Good for probing questions that preoccupy key groups of employees, such as morale issues among front-line production or service workers. Convening groups of people also lets you see how they interact and who exhibits leadership. Fostering discussion promotes deeper insight.
Decision-making case studies	Used to assess decision-making patterns and to identify sources of power and influence. Select an important recent decision and probe how it was made—who participated, and who exerted influence at each stage—by talking to the people involved, probing their perceptions, and noting what is said and unsaid.
Process analysis	Good for examining interactions among departments or functions and assessing the efficiency of key processes. Select a crucial business process, such as delivery of products to customers or distributors, and assign a cross-functional group to chart the process and identify key issues.
Market and plant tours	Opportunities to meet customers and key sales and production personnel informally. Customers' complaints and insights can point up problems and opportunities. Meetings with sales and production staff will help you assess technical capabilities.
Pilot projects	Can yield deep insight into technical capabilities, culture, and politics. Though not the primary purpose of pilot projects, you can learn a lot from how the organization responds to your pilot initiatives.

Copyright ©2001 by Harvard Business School Publishing. All rights reserved.

THIS PAGE INTENTIONALLY LEFT BLANK

Planning to learn

Look back at the first-week learning priorities you specified on page 26. How will you go about meeting those goals? Use the space below to plan how you will gather targeted information about your new organization. If you have already begun your new job, spell out your current learning priorities.

Learning plan for the first week

_____

_____

_____

_____

_____

_____

_____

_____

_____

_____

_____

_____

_____

_____

Copyright ©2001 by Harvard Business School Publishing. All rights reserved.

THIS PAGE INTENTIONALLY LEFT BLANK

THE INFLUENCE CHALLENGE

Learning is essential, but it's not enough. Your efforts won't come to fruition unless you also meet the influence challenge by building credibility, cultivating productive working relationships, and creating supportive internal and external coalitions. Key people must come to believe that you can lead the organization to a desirable future. Their early assessments may well determine whether you build (or lose) credibility. They will be asking:

❑ Do you have the insight and steadiness to make tough decisions about how the organization should proceed next?

❑ Do you represent an attractive set of personal values that people relate to, admire, and seek to emulate?

❑ Do you bring the right kind of energy to the organization, demanding high levels of performance from yourself and everyone else?

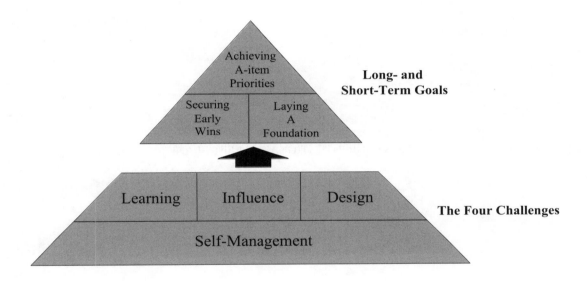

Copyright ©2001 by Harvard Business School Publishing. All rights reserved.

THIS PAGE INTENTIONALLY LEFT BLANK

The transition social system

You aren't the only one going through a transition. As illustrated below, you are part of a *transition social system*: to varying degrees, your transition impacts everyone in the system. Subordinates and employees will have to adjust to your style and expectations, and may be apprehensive about your arrival. Your new boss may have strong ideas about what you need to do, and possibly a very different style. And your success may be dependent on people outside your direct line of command—peers and key external constituencies such as customers, suppliers, and distributors—with whom you have no relationship capital.

You can begin to define your influence goals for each of these groups by answering the following questions:

- ❑ What do I want to achieve with each group?

- ❑ What will my initial priorities be?

- ❑ How can I most effectively exert influence?

In the past where have you been most and least effective in building relationships in the transition social system?

_____

_____

_____

_____

Copyright ©2001 by Harvard Business School Publishing. All rights reserved.

Building and losing credibility

Personal credibility is necessary to build productive working relationships with everyone in the transition social system: your boss, subordinates, peers, other employees, and key external constituencies. With rare exceptions, credibility is neither built nor lost in an hour or a day. It emerges from others' initial assessments of your patterns of conduct: what you say, what you do, and the relationship between the two. Are you consistent? Can your word be trusted? Early in your transition, people will be straining to take your measure and dissect your every move. Once they make up their minds, their opinions will tend to solidify and be difficult to change.

Think about individuals you have observed in new leadership positions. How have you seen new leaders lose credibility and undermine their own effectiveness?

_____

_____

_____

_____

_____

How have you seen new leaders build credibility and leverage themselves at the outset?

_____

_____

_____

_____

_____

Drivers of credibility

There is no recipe for building credibility, but certain basic principles can help guide your early actions. In general, new leaders are perceived as more credible when they are:

- *Demanding but capable of being satisfied.* Effective new leaders press people to make realistic commitments, and then hold their feet to the fire. A low tolerance for failure to meet commitments encourages people to make realistic promises. But if you are never satisfied, people will be sapped of motivation.

- *Accessible but not too familiar.* Being accessible doesn't mean making yourself available indiscriminately. It means being approachable, but in such a way that your authority isn't undermined.

- *Decisive but judicious.* New leaders want to establish their ability to take charge. But appearing impulsive will get you in trouble. Early on, your goal should be to project decisiveness while deferring crucial decisions until you know more.

- *Focused but flexible.* A vicious circle can result if you come across as inflexible and unwilling to consider more than one way to solve a problem. Effective new leaders establish their authority while encouraging input and consultation.

- *Active without causing commotion.* There is a fine line between getting things moving and overwhelming the organization. Leaders must be active without appearing unfocused or pressing people to the point of burnout.

- *Willing to make tough calls but humane.* Most new leaders inherit at least one subordinate who needs to be replaced, requiring an early tough call. Effective new leaders don't shy away from doing what needs to be done; evasion sends a bad message. The key is to do so in ways that are perceived as fair and that preserve the dignity of those involved.

You won't necessarily need to exhibit all these traits to be effective. The drivers of credibility are determined partially by culture, and thus vary from organization to organization. But this list can serve as a reference point for your thinking about building personal credibility.

Copyright ©2001 by Harvard Business School Publishing. All rights reserved.

THIS PAGE INTENTIONALLY LEFT BLANK

Assessing yourself

Take a few minutes to rate yourself on the criteria discussed above.

To what extent am I:

Credibility driver	Assessment
Demanding but capable of being satisfied	1---------2---------3---------4---------5 low high
Accessible but not too familiar	1---------2---------3---------4---------5 low high
Decisive but judicious	1---------2---------3---------4---------5 low high
Focused but flexible	1---------2---------3---------4---------5 low high
Active without causing commotion	1---------2---------3---------4---------5 low high
Willing to make tough calls but humane	1---------2---------3---------4---------5 low high

Now look at your trusted advisors' responses to the same questions in the Observer Assessments (see page 174). If your assessment and theirs are different, why do you think this is the case? In light of these assessments, what will you try to do differently in the interests of building personal credibility?

_____

_____

_____

_____

_____

Copyright ©2001 by Harvard Business School Publishing. All rights reserved.

THIS PAGE INTENTIONALLY LEFT BLANK

Coalition building

The starting point is to think about building supportive coalitions both *internally* (within your own organization or unit) and *externally* in the larger organization and outside. Even when you have formal authority over members of internal groups, you need to build coalitions to support your initiatives. In your dealings with key outside players, coalition building is even more important

Building internal coalitions

If you are to build a critical mass of support for your initiatives, powerful individuals and groups must see it as in their own interests to help you realize your goals. This is why you ignore the politics of organizations at your peril. At the same time, you don't want to be perceived as "political" in the sense of playing favorites or resorting to manipulation. Political networks—informal bonds of solidarity among individuals and groups—can marshal the power either to resist change or to get things done. It's up to you to *build winning coalitions* in support of needed change.

Step 1. Map influence networks.

Employees are embedded in networks of influence and information-sharing. Faced with difficult choices, people often look to others whose opinions they respect for clues about "right thinking." The first step is to analyze these *influence networks*—to trace who defers to whom on crucial issues. Your analysis should also identify *opinion leaders* who exert disproportionate influence. Convincing these pivotal individuals of the need for change translates into broad acceptance, and resistance on their part could galvanize broad opposition. Patterns of deference can be illustrated in the form of an influence diagram.

This influence map traces relationships among members of a hypothetical top-management team. Paul is the CEO, Todd is the VP of Marketing and a long-time ally of Paul's. Nathan and Sarah are VPs of Sales and R&D, respectively. It is Dana, the new Chief Operating Officer, who is performing the analysis. The direction of the arrows indicates the flow of influence. Their width indicates the extent of influence. Note that influence can flow both ways, depending on the issue in question.

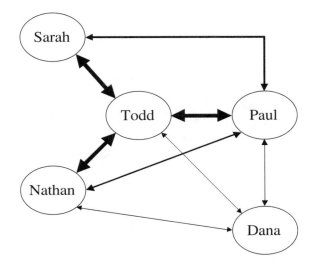

Copyright ©2001 by Harvard Business School Publishing. All rights reserved.

THIS PAGE INTENTIONALLY LEFT BLANK

Use the space provided below to diagram your working understanding of influence relationships among your subordinates. If you can't yet draw such a map, how do you intend to acquire the insight to do so?

Copyright ©2001 by Harvard Business School Publishing. All rights reserved.

THIS PAGE INTENTIONALLY LEFT BLANK

Once you have acquired a solid grasp of key relationships, you can continue to craft your internal coalition-building strategy:

Step 2. Assess individuals' sources of power.

Assessing pivotal individuals' sources of power is a matter of identifying the resources at their command and the people who defer to them. What makes these people influential? How deep and broad is their support? Common sources of power include expertise, control of information, control of resources such as budgets, and loyalty rooted in longstanding supportive relationships.

Step 3. Identify supporters, opponents, and convincibles.

Some people will endorse your agenda right away because it advances their own interests. Other important players will oppose your efforts whatever you do.   Because persuasion consumes valuable time and emotional energy that shouldn't be wasted on the irrevocably opposed, it is essential to figure out promptly who can be persuaded and to direct your efforts accordingly.

Focus on a specific initiative you want to implement early on. Use the table below to identify supporters, opponents, and convincibles.

Supporters	Opponents	Convincibles

Now think through how you will test your hypotheses about support and opposition. Then begin to plot out a strategy for persuading the convincibles.

Copyright ©2001 by Harvard Business School Publishing. All rights reserved.

Step 4. Analyze interests.

Having singled out the convincibles, the next step is to zero in on their *interests* and to craft persuasive arguments. What might prompt them to resist change? The threat of losing a comfortable status quo? Loss of status or a sense of competence? A perceived threat to cherished values? How might such individuals come to see their interests as compatible with yours? How could you help them advance agendas they care about? What motivational drives can you tap into?

With reference to the change initiative you identified above, what do you see as the prime reasons why undecideds might ultimately decide to support or resist you?

Reasons for support	Reasons for resistance

Step 5. Develop a sequencing plan.

The order in which you approach potential allies can have a decisive impact in coalition building. Once you have one ally, it typically becomes easier to recruit others. As you recruit more allies, your resource base grows and your likelihood of prevailing increases, making it easier to recruit still more supporters. This rule of thumb can serve as the basis for a careful *sequencing plan* that spells out the order in which you will approach people to build support.

Use the blank lines below to identify the allies you need most. Think carefully about the sequence in which you will pursue their support, by assessing which early allies would help most to generate further support.

❑ _____

❑ _____

❑ _____

❑ _____

❑ _____

Building external coalitions

Your success is likely to depend on people over whom you have no direct authority, including peers and key external stakeholders such as customers, suppliers, and distributors. Precisely because you lack direct authority over these people, coalition building is even more important with them than it is internally. It is critical to identify the most valuable potential allies and to focus on developing those relationships.

Do your external coalitional analysis the same way you did it internally, first identifying the most important external players.

Step 1. Identify key external players.

Figure out who outside your immediate unit (within the organization or among external constituencies) is critical to your success. List the top five individuals or groups in the table below.

Step 2. Analyze interests.

Now assess the interests of these individuals or groups. Where do your interests coincide and where do they differ? How can you help advance goals that are important to them?

External individuals or groups	Interests

Copyright ©2001 by Harvard Business School Publishing. All rights reserved.

Step 3. Map external influence networks.

Does anyone with whom you are influential exert influence over these individuals or groups? To whom do these external people defer or turn for advice? Use the space below to map out at least one external influence network.

Step 4. Establish your priorities.

What do you need to do to strengthen these relationships? On whom should you focus early? Who can wait? Use the space below to work out your external coalition-building priorities.

_____

_____

_____

_____

_____

_____

_____

_____

_____

_____

Step 5. Develop your sequencing plan.

In what order will you approach people to build external coalitions? Use the blank lines below to specify the sequence in which you will seek external support.

- ❑ _____
- ❑ _____
- ❑ _____
- ❑ _____
- ❑ _____

Copyright ©2001 by Harvard Business School Publishing. All rights reserved.

THIS PAGE INTENTIONALLY LEFT BLANK

Working with your new boss

Your new boss will have more impact than anyone else over whether you succeed or fail. Your boss establishes benchmarks for your success, interprets your actions for other key players, and controls resources you need. Building a productive working relationship with him or her while you establish your mandate and negotiate for resources is a clear early priority.

Defining your goals

When you think about working with your new boss, keep the following goals in mind:

❏ *Clarify mutual expectations early.* Begin managing expectations right away. You are in trouble if your boss expects you to fix things fast when you know that the business has serious structural problems. So it is wise to get bad news on the table early and to lower unrealistic expectations. Be careful to assess your new organization's capacity for change before making ironclad commitments to your new boss.

❏ *Secure commitments for the resources you need.* In conjunction with establishing goals, begin to negotiate for the key resources—people, funding, and knowledge—you need to succeed. Don't commit to goals without getting corresponding commitments on resources. Otherwise you won't have much bargaining power.

❏ *Aim for early wins in areas important to the boss.* Whatever your own priorities, identify what the boss cares about most and pursue results in those areas. That way, your boss will feel some ownership of your success. But don't make the mistake of doing things you consider misguided or trivial. In part, your job is to shape your boss's perceptions of what can and should be achieved.

❏ *Aim for good marks from those whose opinions your boss respects.* This is an aspect of building supportive internal coalitions. Your boss may have pre-existing relationships with people who are now your subordinates. If so, their assessments of you will take on additional importance.

Establishing how you will work together

It's essential to figure out how you and your boss will work together. Your preferences may differ, such as over how much information the boss wants (and you want to give) and how involved the boss wants to be (and you want him or her to be) in the details of what you are doing. Rather than allowing misunderstandings to complicate your relationship, spend some time at the start discussing how you will work together. Even if you don't develop a close personal bond, doing so will help you create a productive working relationship.

Copyright ©2001 by Harvard Business School Publishing. All rights reserved.

Matching your requests for support to your situation

The type of support you need from your boss will vary depending on the business situation you are facing. The role of the boss in a startup is very different than in turnaround, realignment, or sustaining success situations. So you need to gain consensus on the type of situation. Then you have to think carefully about what role you would like your new boss to play and what kinds of support you will ask for.

The table below summarizes typical roles that new bosses play in each of the four major types of transition situations.

Situation	Typical Roles for the New Boss
Startup	❑ Helping to get critically important resources quickly. ❑ Setting clear, measurable goals. ❑ Lots of up-front attention, then get out of the way. ❑ Guidance at key strategic breakpoints. ❑ Help in staying focused.
Turnaround	❑ Same as startup plus: ❑ More support for making and implementing the tough personnel calls ❑ Support for changing or correcting the external image of the organization and its people ❑ Helping the new leader cut deep enough early enough.
Realignment	❑ Same as startup plus: ❑ Helping the new leader make the case for change to the organization, especially if he or she coming in from outside.
Sustaining Success	❑ Constant reality testing: is this truly a sustaining success situation or a realignment? ❑ Support for playing good defense, not making mistakes that damage the business. ❑ Help in finding ways to take the business to a new level.

Living by the golden rule

Do unto others as you would have them do unto you. You will almost certainly hire new people as your subordinates. Just as you need to develop a productive relationship with your new boss, they need to work effectively with you. In the past, have you done a good job of helping subordinates make their own transitions? What might you do differently this time?

_____

_____

_____

Planning for five conversations

Your relationship with your new boss will be built through a series of conversations. These conversations begin before you accept the new position and continue through the time before entry and on into your transition. It is critically important that you cover certain fundamental subjects in these conversations. In fact, it is worth planning for five distinct conversations with your new boss:

❏ The *situational diagnosis conversation.* In this conversation you seek to understand how your new boss sees the business situation. Is it a turnaround or a startup or a realignment or a sustaining success situation? How did the organization get to this point? What are the relevant factors – both soft and hard – that make this a challenge? What resources within the organization do you have to draw upon? Naturally your view may be different than your boss's, but it essential that you understand how he or she sees the situation.

❏ The *expectations conversation.* In this conversation you seek to understand and negotiate expectations. What are the few key things that your new boss needs you to accomplish in the short term and medium term? What will constitute success? When? How will it be measured? Here again, you may come to believe that your boss's expectations are unrealistic and have to work to reset them. Also you should take care, as part of your broader effort to secure early wins, to under-promise and over-deliver.

❏ The *style conversation.* In this conversation you work to understand how you and your new boss can best interact on an ongoing basis. How does she prefer to be communicated with? Face-to-face? In writing? By voice mail or e-mail? How often? What kinds of decisions does he want to be involved in and where can you make the call on your own? How do your styles differ and what are the implications for how you should interact?

❏ The *resources conversation.* In this conversation you negotiate for critical resources. What is it that you need to be successful? What do you need your boss to do? The resources in question need not be funding or personnel. In a realignment situation, for example, you boss can play a critical role in helping you get the organization to confront the need for change.

❏ The *personal development conversation.* Finally, you need to discuss how your time in this job will contribute to your personal development. Are there projects or special assignments that you could get involved in (without sacrificing focus)? Are there courses or programs that would strengthen your capabilities?

In practice, these five conversations are interwoven and take place over time. But there is a sequential logic. Early conversations should focus on situational diagnosis, expectations, and style. As you learn more, you can move to resources, revisiting situation and expectations as necessary. When you feel the relationship is reasonably well-established, you can begin the personal development conversation.

In developing relationships with previous new bosses, which of these five conversations have you conducted well? Which have proven to be problematic? What will you do differently this time?

_____

_____

Copyright ©2001 by Harvard Business School Publishing. All rights reserved.

THIS PAGE INTENTIONALLY LEFT BLANK

Assessing your relationship

Based on what you know now about your new boss, answer the following questions:

What is your current understanding of your boss's expectations? What would you have to do to succeed in his or her eyes? By when?

_____

_____

_____

How does your boss's style differ from your own? Look at your assessment of your own style in the Assessment of Leadership Style beginning on page 163. Then, to the best of your ability, fill it out for your boss. How much information does she want? When and in what form? How does your new boss prefer to learn? To communicate? To motivate? To make decisions?

_____

_____

_____

What role does your boss want to play during the transition period?

_____

_____

_____

How will you get on your boss's agenda? How will you communicate what you need?

_____

_____

_____

Copyright ©2001 by Harvard Business School Publishing. All rights reserved.

Planning for your next meeting

Think about your interactions with your new boss so far. On the basis of these experiences and your assessments of your own and your boss's styles and preferences, draw up an agenda for your next meeting.

_____

_____

_____

_____

_____

Now think about the meeting from your boss's point of view. What is his or her agenda likely to be? If it's different from yours, why? What are the likely implications of this difference?

_____

_____

_____

_____

_____

Finally, think about the key messages you want to convey *in the first few minutes of the meeting*. It's essential for you to drive this conversation. What impressions do you want to create? How are you going to do so?

_____

_____

_____

_____

Establishing your influence priorities

To succeed you have to influence key people in your transition social system. Having analyzed internal and external coalitions, thought through how you will build credibility and assessed your relationship with your new boss, you are now ready to integrate and prioritize your influence goals. Use the table below to outline the objectives you hope to reach by the end of your first few months on the job, referring back as necessary to previous worksheets in this section.

Audience	Influence goals
Subordinates	
Other employees	
Peers	
Outside constituencies	
New boss	

Planning for your first week

What are your priorities for exerting influence and building relationships during your first week? (If you are already on the job, what would you do differently the next time?)

_____

_____

_____

_____

Copyright ©2001 by Harvard Business School Publishing. All rights reserved.

THIS PAGE INTENTIONALLY LEFT BLANK

THE DESIGN CHALLENGE

Success in meeting the learning and influence challenges gives you the knowledge and political capital you need to meet the design challenge. The design challenge has to do with your role as *architect* of the strategy, structure, systems, and skills of your new organization. Even the most charismatic leader can't hope to accomplish much if the strategy is wrong, or the structure misdirects employees' attention (or, worse, contributes to conflict), or key processes and systems are inefficient or unreliable, or the skills of the organization are inadequate for the tasks at hand.

The design challenge is also about your efforts to shape the *work culture*. The most important business problems you face will almost certainly have a culture-change dimension. You have to equip yourself to diagnose the existing culture and to begin molding it into what you need it to be.

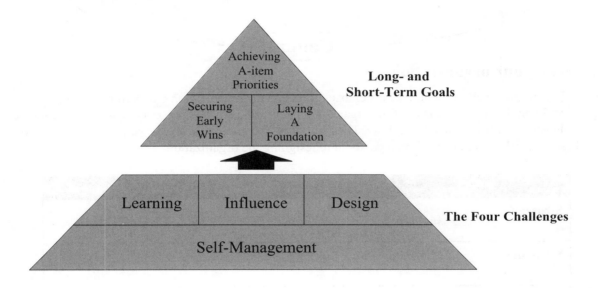

Note: If you are in a startup situation, you will be designing, rather than redesigning, the organization. The material in the following pages is still essential, but will call for you to shift the focus from assessment to design.

Copyright ©2001 by Harvard Business School Publishing. All rights reserved.

Your goal: Achieving alignment

Your overarching design goal is to align the organization's strategy, structure, systems, skills, and work culture. You will have obvious problems if strategy isn't adequate to meet the needs of customers and the challenges of competitors. But mismatches between strategy and structure, structure and systems, systems and skills are equally problematic.

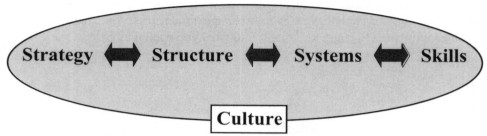

Assessing your organization

Before digging into each element, take a step back to assess the organization's overall pattern of alignment. Even though your grasp of the organization may still be partial, assess the need for change in each dimension and fill in the table below. Then start thinking about how to test your hypotheses. If your hypotheses are validated, how will you go about redesigning the organization?

	Your assessment of the need for change
Strategy	1----------2----------3----------4----------5 low high
Structure	1----------2----------3----------4----------5 low high
Systems/business processes	1----------2----------3----------4----------5 low high
Skills/technologies	1----------2----------3----------4----------5 low high

Now think about the current alignment <u>among</u> these elements. To what extent does the structure support the strategy? Are systems or skills misaligned with structure or strategy?

_____

_____

_____

_____

Assessing and designing strategy

Your starting point ought to be an assessment of the adequacy and coherence of the organization's strategy, both its *stated strategy*—what the organization says it is trying to do—and its *de facto strategy* as revealed in what people are actually doing.

Assessing stated strategy

Much has been written about industry analysis, competitive positioning, and sources of competitive advantage. Though we will not address it here, such analysis is useful to any new leader. But beyond strategic position and driving forces, it is vital to assess the coherence and adequacy of the organization's stated strategy as reflected in its strategic and operating plans.

The coherence test

The coherence test probes the extent to which the stated strategy has a defensible logic. How can you tell? Start by looking at documents that describe the strategy. Then disassemble this strategy into its main pieces—markets, products, technologies, functional plans, goals—and array them side by side to see how they relate to each other. The following questions are diagnostic:

- ❑ Is there a logical thread that continues from one part of the strategy to another?
- ❑ When you compare the analysis of market forces to the five-year objectives, is there an obvious connection?
- ❑ Does the five-year new-product-development budget jibe with the capital investments projected in the operations part of the strategy?
- ❑ Is planned investment in the sales force consistent with the market segments judged most likely to grow?
- ❑ Are plans in place to prepare the sales force for new products in the pipeline?
- ❑ If the strategy suggests that the marketplace is shifting in a new direction, is there a procedure in place to attract and train people to keep the company ahead of those shifts?
- ❑ Is the information-technology investment sufficient to keep pace with the systems change that the strategy will require?

Such threads are not difficult to follow when the strategy has been well thought through. They will not be evident if the strategy lacks logic.

Copyright ©2001 by Harvard Business School Publishing. All rights reserved.

THIS PAGE INTENTIONALLY LEFT BLANK

Summarize your key insights about the coherence of the organization's stated strategy:

_____

_____

_____

_____

_____

_____

_____

_____

_____

_____

_____

_____

_____

_____

_____

_____

_____

Copyright ©2001 by Harvard Business School Publishing. All rights reserved.

THIS PAGE INTENTIONALLY LEFT BLANK

The adequacy test

The strategy may be well thought through and logically integrated, but is it sufficient for what the organization needs to accomplish in the next two to three years? You should ask the following diagnostic questions to assess the adequacy of the stated strategy.

- ❑ Will the toughest external evaluators (bosses, boards of directors, analysts) be convinced that the strategy will provide enough return for the costs and effort expended?
- ❑ Are there plans in place to secure, develop, or maintain enough resources?
- ❑ Are the profit targets over time high enough? Is enough money earmarked for capital investment? For research?

A standard SWOT (strengths, weaknesses, opportunities, and threats) analysis provides a useful point of departure for evaluating the adequacy of the existing strategy. Use the grid below to make an initial assessment of your new organization's strengths and weaknesses, as well as the key opportunities and threats it faces:

Strengths	**Opportunities**
Weaknesses	**Threats**

Copyright ©2001 by Harvard Business School Publishing. All rights reserved.

THIS PAGE INTENTIONALLY LEFT BLANK

Summarize your key insights about the adequacy of the organization's stated strategy:

_____

_____

_____

_____

_____

_____

_____

_____

_____

_____

_____

_____

_____

_____

_____

_____

_____

_____

_____

Copyright ©2001 by Harvard Business School Publishing. All rights reserved.

THIS PAGE INTENTIONALLY LEFT BLANK

Assessing the de facto strategy

Comparing the stated strategy to the organization's apparent de facto strategy calls for looking at how people are actually behaving – what they are <u>doing</u>, not what they are saying. From close observation, you can pinpoint the de facto strategy and assess how it matches up with the stated strategy.

The following diagnostic questions provide a starting point for assessing the de facto strategy:

- ❑ Are the dimensions of performance that management tracks regularly consistent with the explicit or implied emphasis of the strategy? If not, why not? What goals does the organization seem to be pursuing?
- ❑ If the strategy requires teamwork and cross-functional integration, are people trying to act accordingly? If not, why not?
- ❑ If the strategy requires new employee skills, is a training-and-development infrastructure in place to develop those skills?
- ❑ If market-share growth requires being a low-cost producer, is an appropriate base in place for the combination of cost reduction, delivery capability, and speed?

In what ways does the de facto strategy appear to differ from the stated strategy? Why is this the case?

_____

_____

_____

If there are mismatches, is the stated strategy wrong? Or has it not been implemented properly?

_____

_____

_____

What does your assessment suggest about needed changes in the organization's strategy?

_____

_____

_____

Copyright ©2001 by Harvard Business School Publishing. All rights reserved.

THIS PAGE INTENTIONALLY LEFT BLANK

Designing organizational structure

Now that you better understand the organization's strategy and the kinds of changes you need to make, you can turn your attention to structural design.

In designing structure, you function as the architect of four key elements of the organization:

- *Units*: Grouping people with similar and/or complementary expertise, such as by functions, products, or geographical areas. Are the right people in the right places?

- *Decision rights*: Permitting employees to make specified decisions on behalf of the organization. Are decisions made at the right level?

- *Performance-measurement and reward systems*: Measuring and rewarding performance in ways that encourage employees to make the right decisions. Are employees' interests aligned with those of the organization's shareholders?

- *Reporting relationships*: Establishing channels and processes for monitoring and control, information sharing, and high-level decision making. Are the organization's needs for integration and accountability in balance?

Assessing the structure

Take some time to think about the existing structure of the organization. How are the major units organized? How have decision rights been allocated? How is performance measured, and how are results rewarded or punished? How do reporting relationships work? Use the space below to identify the most salient features of the organization's design.

_____

_____

_____

_____

_____

_____

_____

_____

_____

Copyright ©2001 by Harvard Business School Publishing. All rights reserved.

Common structural problems

For each of the four main structural elements of an organization—units, decision rights, measurement and reward schemes, and reporting relationships—there are corresponding ways in which poor design decisions undermine the potential for high performance. Each pitfall is associated with a corresponding *core tradeoff* that must be made as you design the organization.

Problem 1. Units' knowledge bases are too narrow or too shallow. When you group together people with similar knowledge and capabilities they can develop their collective knowledge base, creating deep wells of expertise about, for example, how to develop a particular type of product. But if units' knowledge bases are too narrow, isolation and compartmentalization can result. Units with a broad mix of skills, on the other hand, may result in more knowledge integration at the cost of less deep expertise.

Problem 2. Employees' scope for decision making is too narrow or too broad. It's a fundamental principle of organizational design that *decisions should be made by the people who are best equipped, in terms of relevant knowledge, to make them.* If your organization is overly centralized, too many decisions are made by people who lack the relevant knowledge possessed by others lower in the organization. This structure contributes to overload at the upper levels and bad decisions. But lower-level people who are given too much scope to make decisions may fail to understand the larger implications and sub-optimize.

Problem 3. Employees are under- or over-rewarded. An equally fundamental design principle is to *seek to align the interests of every individual decision-maker with the interests of the organization as a whole.* This is why, for example, stock-option grants have become such a central component of corporate compensation plans: they focus everyone on creating shareholder value. Measurement and compensation schemes create problems when employees are insufficiently rewarded for their individual or collective efforts. Problems also arise when efforts are rewarded that advance employees' own interests or those of their units at the expense of broader organizational goals—such as when multiple product groups could serve the same set of customers but lack incentives to cooperate.

Problem 4. Reporting relationships lead to compartmentalization or diffusion of accountability. Reporting relationships serve the need for senior management to monitor and control the workings of the organization. Hierarchical reporting relationships (with reasonable spans of control) contribute to straightforward assignment of line responsibility and accountability. But they also can lead to compartmentalization and poor information sharing. More complex reporting arrangements, such as matrix structures, broaden information sharing and reduce compartmentalization but can lead to diffusion of accountability.

Which of these structural problems, if any, is most prominent in your organization?

_____

_____

_____

_____

Aligning structure and strategy

The organization's structure must support its strategy. If you plan to change the strategy, what kinds of supporting structural changes will you need to make? Draw on your knowledge of the organization to fill out the table below.

Design element	Need for change
How employees are grouped into units	1----------2----------3----------4----------5 low high
How decision rights are allocated	1----------2----------3----------4----------5 low high
How performance is measured and rewarded	1----------2----------3----------4----------5 low high
How reporting relationships are structured	1----------2----------3----------4----------5 low high

Establishing structural change priorities

Given what you know now, what do you think your highest priorities will be for changing the organization's structure? When do you think you will begin to make those changes?

_____

_____

_____

_____

_____

_____

_____

_____

_____

Copyright ©2001 by Harvard Business School Publishing. All rights reserved.

THIS PAGE INTENTIONALLY LEFT BLANK

Designing systems

Systems are the core processes through which your organization transforms information, materials, and knowledge into products and services. They link the units that compose the organization's structure. It is essential to achieve alignment between structure (how key units are defined) and systems (the core processes that link the units).

The fundamental question to ask is whether the organization's systems will permit it to meet the demands posed by the strategy. Are existing processes capable of meeting and exceeding the requirements of customers, employees, and managers? A representative list of core business processes for a credit-card company appears below.

Business processes	Support-service processes	Production and service-delivery processes
❑ Strategic planning	❑ Collections	❑ Application processing
❑ Business planning	❑ Customer acquisition	❑ Authorizations management
❑ Budgeting	❑ Financial management	❑ Billing
❑ Quality management	❑ Human-resource management	❑ Credit-card production
	❑ Information and technology management	❑ Credit screening
	❑ Relationship management	❑ Customer inquiry
		❑ Payment processing
		❑ Transaction processing

Identifying core processes

Use the table below to identify the most important business processes in your organization.

Business processes	Support-service processes	Production and service-delivery processes

Copyright ©2001 by Harvard Business School Publishing. All rights reserved.

Assessing process performance

Next, prioritize the processes you identified above in terms of need for improvement. This means digging into their productivity, timeliness, reliability, and quality. Use the table below to identify the seven highest-priority business processes and the dimensions of their performance most in need of improvement.

Core process	Priorities for improvement			
1.	productivity	timeliness	reliability	quality
2.	productivity	timeliness	reliability	quality
3.	productivity	timeliness	reliability	quality
4.	productivity	timeliness	reliability	quality
5.	productivity	timeliness	reliability	quality
6.	productivity	timeliness	reliability	quality
7.	productivity	timeliness	reliability	quality

Establishing process improvement priorities

The next step is to establish priorities for process improvement. It is useful to think about improving your organization's core processes in terms of a portfolio of radical and incremental improvement projects. Some processes will be candidates for radical improvement through process reengineering; others will be better suited to incremental continuous-improvement methodologies. Keep in mind the following two cautions:

❑ You can't hope to fundamentally reengineer more than a couple of core business processes at a time, because the organization won't be able to cope with so much change. Continuous-improvement projects are inherently less disruptive, but they can't achieve breakthrough results.

❑ Don't simply automate troubled processes, because doing so rarely solves the underlying problems. Nor does it realize much of the potential performance gain.

Which of your new organization's core business processes appear to be good candidates for radical redesign?

_____

_____

_____

_____

_____

Which processes are candidates for continuous-improvement projects?

_____

_____

_____

_____

_____

Copyright ©2001 by Harvard Business School Publishing. All rights reserved.

What are your priorities for process improvement during your transition?

_____

_____

_____

_____

_____

_____

Analyzing and improving processes

We will not discuss resources and methods for improving business processes in detail. But it is worth highlighting a powerful tool and some ideas that you can use to improve critical processes.

Process mapping is straightforward diagramming of business processes in terms of tasks, organizational units, and interfaces. A team of representatives from the units responsible for each stage of the target process maps out the process flow from beginning to end. The team should look for *bottlenecks* and *problem interfaces* between units responsible for adjacent sets of tasks; process failures often occur at these handoffs. The team should also be asked to identify the highest-potential improvements. The result is usually a substantial increase in overall understanding of the process and its problems.

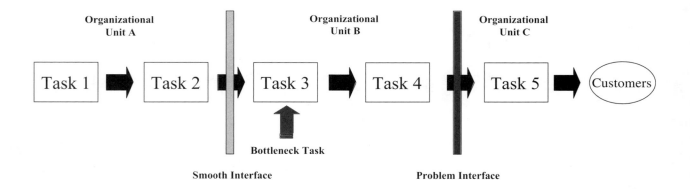

Assessing and developing skills

Your next focus will be the organization's base of skills and knowledge. Here the basic question is: Do the existing capabilities of the organization match the skills necessary to achieve outstanding performance in key business processes?

Assessing the existing skill base

While the specifics of your appraisal depend on the organization's history and the nature of its business, these questions will help you assess your organization's strengths, vulnerabilities, and flexibility:

On knowledge

- ❑ Do employees have the expertise to sustain high performance?
- ❑ If not, what is the best way to acquire those skills?

On technologies

- ❑ What are the core technologies on which the company's equity, reputation, and industry standing depend?
- ❑ Do these core technologies match those the strategy calls for?
- ❑ Does the strategy call for a change in the technologies that built the company's reputation?

On the history of investment

- ❑ What is the history of investments to strengthen the company's technology base? How has their effectiveness been measured?
- ❑ Has the technical-training and education budget grown or shrunk over the past five years?
- ❑ What efforts have been made to ensure that employees stay up-to-date on technical developments?
- ❑ Have budgets for researchers, research equipment, and other technology assets grown at the same pace as volume and profit growth?

On organizational memory

- ❑ Is documentation on key technologies stored in a central location and kept up-to-date?
- ❑ Is it widely accessible?
- ❑ Do employees take advantage of it?

On supporting external affiliations

- ❑ Does the organization have affiliations with research institutions or technology partners?
- ❑ If so, are they the right affiliates?
- ❑ Are they utilized effectively?
- ❑ Are the best people involved?

Identifying gaps and underutilized resources

The ultimate goal of assessing capabilities is to identify gaps and underutilized resources. Where capabilities are inadequate to support the strategy and key processes, or to sustain the necessary rate of improvement, gaps exist. Underutilized resources include technologies that have not been exploited and groups whose expertise has been squandered. Identifying gaps and underutilized resources is a direct contribution to improvements in performance.

Copyright ©2001 by Harvard Business School Publishing. All rights reserved.

THIS PAGE INTENTIONALLY LEFT BLANK

What do you see as the biggest gaps in skills and technological capabilities?

_____

_____

_____

_____

_____

Which of the underutilized resources do you see as most valuable?

_____

_____

_____

_____

_____

Establishing skill-building priorities

What are your priorities for process improvement during the transitional period?

_____

_____

_____

_____

_____

_____

Copyright ©2001 by Harvard Business School Publishing. All rights reserved.

THIS PAGE INTENTIONALLY LEFT BLANK

Shaping the culture

The most important business problems you will face will almost certainly have a cultural dimension. Cultural habits and norms can operate very powerfully to reinforce the status quo. So it is vital to diagnose problems in the existing culture and figure out how to begin molding it in accordance with the organization's needs. These assessments are particularly important if you are coming in from outside or joining a unit with a strong subculture.

The culture iceberg

You can't hope to change your organization's work culture if you don't understand it. It's useful to analyze an organization's work culture at three levels—*symbols, norms,* and *assumptions*—as illustrated below.

- ❑ *Symbols* are visible signs that differentiate one culture from another, including logos and styles of dress. Are there distinctive symbols – official and unofficial – that signify the organization and help members recognize each other?

- ❑ *Norms* are shared social rules that guide "right behavior." What kinds of behavior get rewarded and what elicits scorn or disapproval?

- ❑ *Assumptions* are the often-unarticulated beliefs that pervade and underpin social systems. These beliefs are "the air that everyone breathes." What does everyone take for granted as "truth?"

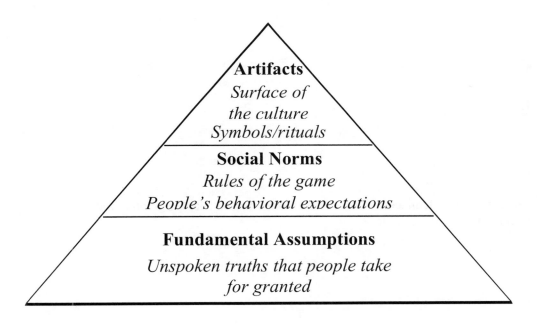

To understand a culture, you must peer below the surface at the assumptions its members take for granted. For a new leader, the most pertinent assumptions involve power and value. With regard to power, the key question is: who do employees think can legitimately exercise authority and make decisions? As a corollary, it is useful to ask: what actions and outcomes do employees believe creates social value? Different assumptions about power and value can complicate efforts to align the organization.

Copyright ©2001 by Harvard Business School Publishing. All rights reserved.

Assessing the culture

Use the space below to identify key features of the organization's culture at each level: symbols, norms, and assumptions. Pay particular attention to assumptions that seem to guide peoples' actions and of which they may be unaware. Keep in mind that you may have to do this analysis for different groups or *subcultures* in the organization.

Symbols. What are distinctive signs and symbols in the organization?

_____

_____

_____

_____

_____

Norms. What are the governing "rules of the game"? What kinds of behavior are tacitly encouraged and discouraged?

_____

_____

_____

_____

_____

Assumptions. What unarticulated truths does everyone seem to take for granted, for example, about how decisions get made or what is valued?

_____

_____

_____

_____

_____

Dysfunctional cultural patterns

Cultural patterns can stand in the way of high performance; some that do are summarized below. Note that an organization can be highly energized but still unfocused and undisciplined. Alternatively, misplaced focus and discipline can come at the expense of an innovative spirit.

Lack of...	Symptoms
Focus	❑ The organization is unable to define its priorities or has too many priorities.
	❑ Resources are spread too thin, leading to frequent crises and "fire-fighting." People are rewarded for their ability to put out fires.
Discipline	❑ Core processes and key people exhibit wide variations in performance.
	❑ Employees don't understand that inconsistency has negative consequences. Failure to meet commitments is excused.
Innovation	❑ Internal benchmarks of performance substitute for a focus on best competitors.
	❑ Generation-to-generation progress in products and processes is slow and incremental.
	❑ Employees are rewarded for maintaining stable performance and not for pushing the envelope.
Teamwork	❑ Competitiveness is directed internally rather than externally.
	❑ Functions vie to protect turf rather than to advance a shared agenda.
	❑ People are rewarded for creating fiefdoms.
Sense of Urgency	❑ External and internal customer needs are ignored.
	❑ Responsiveness is not seen as an important value.
	❑ Complacency is apparent in beliefs like "We're the best and always have been" or "It doesn't matter if we do it right now because it won't make a difference."

To identify aspects of the work culture that may be undermining performance, begin with the following questions:

❑ Are people capable of sustaining attention, establishing priorities, and marshaling a critical mass of resources to pursue them, or are their efforts diffuse and unfocused?

❑ Do key processes and people deliver the necessary performance crisply and consistently, or are wide variations in quality, cost, and speed permitted?

❑ Is internal competition for turf more vigorous and heartfelt than external competition with other companies?

❑ Are innovative products and processes developed and brought to market as nimbly or better than the company's best competitors?

❑ Does an appropriate sense of urgency prevail about pursuing priorities and responding to problems?

Copyright ©2001 by Harvard Business School Publishing. All rights reserved.

Diagnosing cultural problems

Use the space below to assess the extent to which the organization suffers from the problems listed above.

Focus. Do people focus appropriately or are they pulled in too many directions?

_____

_____

_____

Discipline. Are plans made and executed reliably?

_____

_____

_____

Innovation. Can the organization innovate as well as execute?

_____

_____

_____

Teamwork. Are competitive energies directed externally or internally?

_____

_____

_____

Urgency. Does an appropriate sense of urgency prevail?

_____

_____

_____

Approaches to getting started on cultural change during your transition are discussed on pages 151 –152.

THE SELF-MANAGEMENT CHALLENGE

Taking charge successfully calls for more than effectiveness; it also takes a clear head and emotional balance. The stresses of the transition make it imperative that you remain disciplined, energized, and focused while maintaining perspective and exercising good judgment. You will unavoidably experience your transition as demanding and stressful, but there are better and worse ways to cope.

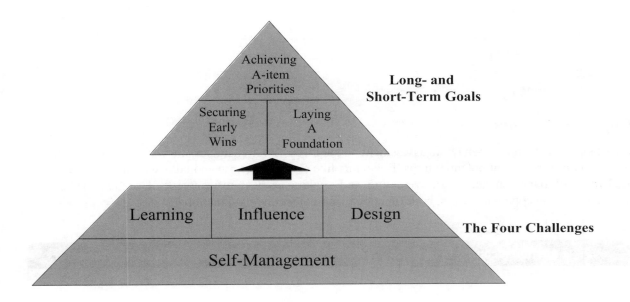

Copyright ©2001 by Harvard Business School Publishing. All rights reserved.

Potential pitfalls

Drawing on your Assessment of Reactions to Stress (see page 167) and the Observer Assessment of Reactions to Stress (see page 177) that you solicited from trusted advisors, identify the three self-management pitfalls to which you are most susceptible.

1. _____

2. _____

3. _____

Coping behaviors

Now look at your coping behaviors assessment on page 169. Your characteristic ways of coping with stress may also represent potential traps. Behaviors like regular exercise and talks with trusted advisors are helpful. Reliance on sleep aids, overeating, and drinking carry significant risks. Use the table below to list the ways you cope with stress, both functional and potentially dysfunctional.

Functional coping behaviors	Potentially dysfunctional coping behaviors

Your family in transition

If your new position involves relocation, your family is also in transition. Your spouse may be making a job transition, too, and your children may have to leave their friends and change schools. In other words, the fabric of your family's life may be disrupted just when you most need their support. The stresses of your professional transition can easily amplify the difficulty of your family's transition. Likewise, family members' difficulties can add to your already heavy emotional load.

Planning for your move

The starting point is to acknowledge that your family may be unhappy, even resentful about the transition. There is no avoiding disruption, but talking about it and working through the sense of loss together can be helpful.

There are a few other things you can do to ease the transition for your family.

❑ *Tap into your company's relocation service*, if there is one, as soon as possible. Corporate relocation services are typically limited to helping you find a new home, move belongings, and locate schools, but such help can make a big difference.

❑ *Analyze your family's existing support system.* Moving severs your ties with all the people who provide essential services for your family: doctors, lawyers, dentists, baby-sitters, tutors, coaches, and more. It's important to recognize this early, do an inventory, identify priorities, and invest in finding replacements quickly. Use the space on the next page to do this.

❑ *Get your spouse back on track, too.* Your spouse may quit his or her old job with the intention of finding a new one after relocating. Unhappiness can fester if the search is slow. To accelerate it, negotiate up front with your company for job-search support or find such support shortly after moving.

❑ *Time the family move carefully.* For children, it is substantially more difficult if they have to move in the middle of a school year. If it is possible to wait until the end of the school year to move your family, it's worth considering. The price, of course, is separation from your loved ones and the wear-and-tear of commuting for you.

❑ *Retain the familiar.* Reestablish familiar family rituals as quickly as possible and maintain them throughout the transition. Help from favorite relatives, such as grandparents, also makes a difference.

❑ *Invest in cultural familiarization.* If you move internationally, get professional advice about the cross-cultural transition. Isolation is a far greater risk for your family if there are language and cultural barriers.

Copyright ©2001 by Harvard Business School Publishing. All rights reserved.

THIS PAGE INTENTIONALLY LEFT BLANK

Building your family's support system

Use the space below to list the support relationships you will have to rebuild after moving. Which are your highest priorities?

_____

_____

_____

_____

_____

_____

_____

_____

_____

_____

_____

_____

_____

_____

_____

_____

_____

_____

_____

_____

Copyright ©2001 by Harvard Business School Publishing. All rights reserved.

THIS PAGE INTENTIONALLY LEFT BLANK

Disciplines of self-awareness

Loss of perspective is common during a transition. Inevitably, you will have to make tough calls without enough information. This is hard at any time, but bad decisions are more likely if you are unaware of your own reactions to the situation you are in. To avoid becoming isolated or losing perspective, look for ways to "go to the balcony," to step back and look at the situation from a higher level.

We have already discussed one crucial aspect of self-diagnosis: understanding your own leadership style and characteristic preferences. Beyond that, two basic disciplines can help you maintain perspective: (1) structured self-assessment and (2) advice and counsel. Structured self-assessment means setting aside time to reflect on what is going on and assess what needs to be done to reflect on the emotional and interpersonal aspects of your situation. The advice and counsel of a network of trusted advisors inside and outside the organization will allow you to talk through what you are experiencing and internalizing.

Copyright ©2001 by Harvard Business School Publishing. All rights reserved.

Engaging in self-assessment

For some new leaders, structured self-assessment involves keeping a daily journal of impressions and questions. For others it means setting aside time each week to assess how things are going. The key is to find an approach that suits your style, and then to discipline yourself to use it regularly and translate the resulting insights into action.

In your self-assessment, watch out for three common self-management traps:

Trap 1. *Mistaking personal blocks for situational blocks*

Are your perceived difficulties the result of your situation or do their sources lie within you? Even experienced and skilled people can fall prey to the tendency to blame problems on the situation they are facing instead of their own actions. Since they feel they have less power to overcome situational blocks than personal blocks, the net effect is that they are not as proactive as they should be.

Trap 2. *Practicing work avoidance*

New leaders tend to gravitate toward problems and tasks they understand and away from those they don't. The experienced marketing executive continues to act as VP of marketing though he now has general management responsibility, or the former COO continues to focus on operational details after being named CEO, avoiding the less familiar challenges of dealing with the press, analysts, investors, and governments. Keep in mind that you can be very busy and still failing. In fact, busyness is a common form of work avoidance—of not grappling with the challenges you really need to face.

Take a few minutes to look back at your assessment of your problem preferences in the Assessment of Leadership Style (see pages 161-162). What does it say about your potential blind spots?

Trap 3. *Suppressing doubts*

Another common reaction to the stresses of taking charge is to repress your doubts and uncertainties in the name of feeling certain and in control. It is unquestionably important to *project* a confident image to employees, but the need to feel in control can lead to suppression of doubts and block learning. New leaders who come in with "the answer" often do so to avoid confronting how much they don't know. They then alienate the people who understand the nuances of the problem, creating a vicious cycle.

These traps are all forms of *denial*: self-deception in the name of maintaining control or avoiding unpleasant truths.

A template for structured reflection

The power of structured reflection is enhanced if you pursue it regularly and are attentive to how things change over time. Consider setting aside 15 minutes at the end or beginning of each week to answer the same set of questions. Save your responses so you can look back regularly at the previous couple of weeks'. You will see patterns develop, both in the problems you face and in your reactions to them.

These questions provide a template for reflecting about your first days in your new job. Take some time to think about them and use the space on the next page to summarize your answers.

What do you feel so far?

- ❏ On a scale of high to low, do you feel:
- ❏ Excited? If not, why not? What have you done to block feeling excited?
- ❏ Confident? If not, why not? What have you done to block feeling confident?
- ❏ Do you feel in control of your success? If not, what do you feel you must do to gain more control?

What has bothered you so far?

- ❏ With whom have you not connected? Why? What did you do to cause that lack of rapport?
- ❏ Of the meetings you have attended, which has been most bothersome? Why?
- ❏ Of all that you have seen or heard, what has disturbed you most?

What has gone well and poorly?

- ❏ Of the interactions you've had, which would you handle differently if you had the chance? Which exceeded your expectations? Why?
- ❏ What decisions have you made that turned out particularly well? Not so well? Why?
- ❏ Of the main missed opportunities, was a better result blocked primarily by you or by something beyond your control?

Meeting the four challenges

- ❏ *Learning*: How are you learning? Is the balance appropriate among technical, cultural, and political learning? What are your priorities for learning?
- ❏ *Influence*: How are you doing at influencing key groups, internally and externally? What coalitions do you most need to build?
- ❏ *Design*: What progress have you made in assessing the strategy and altering it if necessary? In aligning strategy, structure, systems, and skills? What are your priorities?
- ❏ *Self-management*: Have style issues been a problem so far? If so, what can you do about it? Are you using advice and counsel effectively? What are your priorities for building your advice and counsel network?

Copyright ©2001 by Harvard Business School Publishing. All rights reserved.

THIS PAGE INTENTIONALLY LEFT BLANK

Summary of reflections

_____

_____

_____

_____

_____

_____

_____

_____

_____

_____

_____

_____

_____

_____

_____

_____

_____

_____

_____

_____

_____

Note: A blank copy of the structured reflection template is available in Part 6B (see pages 189-191). You should make copies of this template and use it periodically (ideally weekly) to track how you are doing.

Copyright ©2001 by Harvard Business School Publishing. All rights reserved.

THIS PAGE INTENTIONALLY LEFT BLANK

Using advice and counsel

Advice and counsel, though useful for all leaders, can make the difference between success and failure for new leaders. You will benefit from building a strong network of advisors who can make themselves available at crucial times.

Types of advisors and counselors

You should cultivate three types of advisors and counselors: technical advisors, political counselors, and personal counselors.

Technical advisors provide expert analysis of technologies, markets, and strategy:

❑ Suggesting applications for new technologies.

❑ Recommending strategies for entering new markets.

Political counselors help you deal with culture, politics, and relationships within your new organization:

❑ Helping you implement the advice of a technical advisor.

❑ Serving as a sounding board as you think through and test ways to implement your agenda.

❑ Helping you to shape the organization's decision-making process in ways that are compatible with your style.

❑ Challenging you by asking "what-if" questions.

Personal counselors focus on your personal well-being rather than the cultural or political challenges you face:

❑ Offering feedback or advice with an eye to your personal benefit.

❑ Expressing concern about your level of stress or fatigue.

❑ Providing a safe place for you to talk through worries or doubts.

Building a balanced network

The most common causes of failure are not technical; typically, they are political (such as faulty interpretation of political currents) or personal (such as becoming overwhelmed by the internal challenges of the transition). The bottom line is that you are more likely to succeed if you build and utilize a balanced advice network. Gaining such an advantage is a function of finding advisors appropriate to the situation and your style, and learning to be an accomplished consumer of the right kinds of help.

Copyright ©2001 by Harvard Business School Publishing. All rights reserved.

Surveying your advice and counsel network

Fill out the two tables on this page and the top of the next page by doing the following:

A. List your key advisors and counselors, both internal and external.
B. Identify the domains in which each assists you (technical, political, and personal). Check more than one domain if appropriate.
C. Assess the degree to which each relationship helps you become a more effective leader.

Assessing internal advisors and counselors (within your organization)

Advisor/ counselor	Technical	Political	Personal	Value of relationship				
1.				1	2	3	4	5
				Low				High
2.				1	2	3	4	5
				Low				High
3.				1	2	3	4	5
				Low				High
4.				1	2	3	4	5
				Low				High
5.				1	2	3	4	5
				Low				High

Assessing external advisors and counselors (outside your organization)

Advisor/ counselor	Technical	Political	Personal	Value of relationship				
1.				1	2	3	4	5
				Low				High
2.				1	2	3	4	5
				Low				High
3.				1	2	3	4	5
				Low				High
4.				1	2	3	4	5
				Low				High
5.				1	2	3	4	5
				Low				High

Now answer the following questions:

My network gives me the support I need to do my job effectively.

1	2	3	4	5	6	7
Strongly disagree	Disagree	Somewhat disagree	Neither agree nor disagree	Somewhat agree	Agree	Strongly agree

Why or why not?

_____

_____

Copyright ©2001 by Harvard Business School Publishing. All rights reserved.

I have briefed the key people in my network about the organization's situation and my aspirations to transform it.

1	2	3	4	5	6	7
Strongly disagree	Disagree	Somewhat disagree	Neither agree nor disagree	Somewhat agree	Agree	Strongly agree

Why or why not?

_____

_____

The key people in my network understand how I think and how I react to challenges.

1	2	3	4	5	6	7
Strongly disagree	Disagree	Somewhat disagree	Neither agree nor disagree	Somewhat agree	Agree	Strongly agree

Why or why not?

_____

_____

My network will continue to be sufficient to support me in future positions I may take.

1	2	3	4	5	6	7
Strongly Disagree	Disagree	Somewhat Disagree	Neither agree nor disagree	Somewhat Agree	Agree	Strongly Agree

Why or why not?

_____

_____

Establishing network-building priorities

Draw on your assessment to specify priorities for strengthening your network.

_____

_____

_____

_____

_____

_____

_____

_____

_____

_____

_____

_____

_____

_____

_____

_____

Copyright ©2001 by Harvard Business School Publishing. All rights reserved.

THIS PAGE INTENTIONALLY LEFT BLANK

PART THREE: BUILDING MOMENTUM

Roughly by the end of your first month on the job, you should be ready to begin some long- and short-term planning with an eye to building momentum. This part of the workbook will show you how.

PLANNING FOR LONG- AND SHORT-TERM SUCCESS

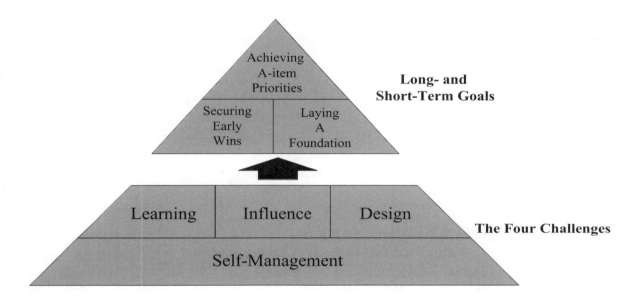

Planning for long-term success

To figure out where to begin, start at the end. Your ultimate objective, as we have discussed, is to end your "era" in the organization—typically two to three years—having exceeded the expectations of those who evaluate your performance and satisfied with your own performance. You lay the groundwork for this long-term success throughout your transition. But early on you should be able to articulate a set of *A-item priorities*. You should also be actively developing a *personal vision* of what you want the organization eventually to become.

Planning for short-term success

Together, your A-item priorities and personal vision will serve as your "guiding star" in establishing shorter-term goals for the remainder of the transitional period. To build momentum, you need to figure out how to get some early wins. At the same time you need to begin lay the foundation for longer-term success by building your team and taking actions to change the culture.

Copyright ©2001 by Harvard Business School Publishing. All rights reserved.

THIS PAGE INTENTIONALLY LEFT BLANK

ESTABLISHING A-ITEM PRIORITIES

When you are confident that you know enough to specify longer-term objectives for the organization, use the space below to identify *at most* seven A-item priorities. Keep in mind that these are goals that you want to achieve within two to three years, not shorter-term goals for the transitional period. Be specific about what will constitute success, identifying particular measures and targets wherever possible. Keep in mind, too, that you will probably modify these goals as you learn more.

1.

2.

3.

4.

5.

6.

7.

Copyright ©2001 by Harvard Business School Publishing. All rights reserved.

THIS PAGE INTENTIONALLY LEFT BLANK

DEVELOPING A PERSONAL VISION

Clear A-item priorities are necessary but not sufficient to guide your choice of short-term goals. You also need a personal vision of what the organization will have become by the end of your tenure. Note that this is a *personal* vision, and not a *shared* vision. You may eventually decide to share elements of it with others and work to establish a common vision, but this is not something to attempt early in your transition. The goal here is a compelling mental image that helps *you* stay on track.

A compelling personal vision has the following attributes:

- ❑ **Consistency with A-item priorities.** The vision must be consistent with the long-term objectives you set for yourself and your organization.

- ❑ **Linkage to core values.** An effective vision is built on a foundation of values, such as integrity and loyalty, that imbue it with meaning and purpose.

- ❑ **Embodiment in evocative descriptors.** A-items and core values must describe in graphic terms the organization as you envision it: how it will be organized and what will be different about it. Launching 12 rockets in 10 years is a goal; putting a man on the moon by the end of the decade is a vision.

Let the image of the future in your mind's eye take shape gradually as you work at your A-item priorities, informed by the situation and by your style and core values. As your personal vision coalesces, you will be able to articulate it in succinct, compelling terms to keep yourself focused (and for eventual presentation to others).

Envisioning your new organization

When you feel you know enough to begin hammering out a personal vision, begin with a thought experiment. Imagine that two years have passed, during which you have worked to transform the organization. Using the space below, describe how the organization will look and feel. How will employees behave differently? What will happen then that isn't happening now? Try to capture these differences in evocative terms, such as "I see employees jumping to respond to customer concerns."

_____

_____

_____

_____

_____

Copyright ©2001 by Harvard Business School Publishing. All rights reserved.

Describing the future

Next, describe what you want the organization to become in terms of the attitudes listed below. How do you want people to feel?

Loyalty	Achievement
❑ Commitment to an ideal ❑ Sacrifice to realize the ideal	❑ Drive for excellence, quality, and continuous improvement ❑ Providing challenging opportunities
Commitment and contribution ❑ Service to customers and suppliers ❑ Creating a better society and a better world ❑ Making commitments and meeting them	**Affiliation** ❑ Teamwork and constant concern for the good of the team ❑ A climate that emphasizes personally rewarding work, especially in groups
Individual worth and dignity ❑ Respect for the individual, expressed as elimination of exploitative/patronizing practices, decency, and opportunity for all ❑ Providing the means for people to reach their potential	**Power** ❑ Quest to be large, dominant, and in control ❑ Rewards, recognition, and status, individually and for the organization
Integrity ❑ Ethical and honest behavior ❑ Fairness in all interactions	

Now think about the future in terms of how work will be structured and how employees will behave. Use the following questions to stimulate your thinking.

Structure of work	Behavior of employees
❑ How will work be structured? ❑ How will information be shared? ❑ What kind of information? With whom? When? ❑ How will products be developed? ❑ How will products be distributed? ❑ What will the product-supply chain look like? ❑ How many suppliers will there be? Where?	❑ How will the company be managed? ❑ How will coordination be handled? ❑ How will big problems be solved? ❑ How will small problems be prevented from becoming big problems? ❑ How will employees participate in problem solving? ❑ What will relationships with customers and suppliers be like? ❑ What will the prevailing style of teamwork be? How will I know? ❑ What will the organizational climate be like? How will I know?

Crafting a personal vision statement

Use the space below to draft a *one-paragraph* provisional statement of your personal vision for the organization.

_____

_____

_____

_____

_____

_____

_____

_____

Refining your vision

You can't develop a full-blown vision in a vacuum. Eventually you will be ready to expose it to testing by others. The key is to decide judiciously with whom you will discuss it and when.

There are obvious risks to revealing your vision prematurely or to the wrong people. If it is perceived as naïve or uninformed about organizational realities, your credibility will suffer. If it potentially conflicts with the boss's vision, perhaps because of his or her preoccupation with legacy, it may be wise to keep it under wraps until you are well established. Likewise, be careful not to engage in collective visioning with your team until you are sure who will be staying. It's demoralizing for everyone to engage in this kind of team-building if you intend to restructure the team.

Use the space below to identify the individuals with whom you will discuss your emerging personal vision first, and roughly when you want to begin.

1. _____

2. _____

3. _____

4. _____

Copyright ©2001 by Harvard Business School Publishing. All rights reserved.

Use the space below to summarize what you have learned in early conversations about your personal vision. What works well and what will need to be modified?

_____

_____

_____

_____

_____

_____

_____

_____

_____

_____

Cultivating a visioning mindset

People differ in their capacity for visioning. But whatever your natural ability, you can get better at it. The goal is to cultivate a visioning mindset—the inclination to look at situations not as they are but as they could be. One simple technique is to spend a few moments visioning whenever you enter a new physical space (an office or a friend's home) or social situation (business meeting, informal get-together with friends, interaction with customers). "Go to the balcony" and ask yourself: how could this space be transformed to better serve the needs of its users? How might this situation be made more productive or enjoyable? What could we do to delight this customer? Try to evoke an image of what could be. Over time, you will internalize this discipline and enhance your capacity for imaginative visualization.

Use the space below to identify opportunities to exercise your visioning skills.

_____

_____

_____

SECURING EARLY WINS

When you start thinking about the long term, begin planning to get some early wins during the first wave of change. Short- and long-term planning in tandem ensures that your pursuit of early wins also advances your A-item priorities and personal vision.

Why do you need early wins?

Within six months you must have energized people and focused them on solving the most pressing problems, using techniques that have a prompt, dramatic impact. It is crucial for employees to perceive momentum as building during the transition. Tangible improvements in performance motivate employees and encourage them to experiment further. Early wins are a powerful way to get your people pumped up.

Guidelines for securing early wins

Early wins call for identifying problems that can be tackled in a brief period of time and whose solutions will yield conspicuous operational and financial (not just behavioral and attitudinal) improvements in performance. Examples include bottlenecks that restrict productivity and misaligned incentive systems that undermine performance by generating conflict. (Team building and improving the effectiveness of meetings, although they might make eventual contributions to the business, are not tangible enough to provide early wins.)

Securing early wins involves three discrete steps:

Step 1. Establish A-item priorities.
Your goals for the transition period grow out of your longer-term A-item priorities. Near-term actions thus do double duty, helping secure early wins that move the organization toward longer-term objectives.

Step 2. Identify centers of gravity.
Your initial assessments of strategy and performance should enable you to identify one or two *centers of gravity*, operational areas, or processes, in which substantial and noticeable early wins can be achieved. Examples are a consumer-goods company's distribution system, a mutual fund's investment process, and a pharmaceutical company's handoff from research to marketing.

Step 3. Initiate pilot projects.
By articulating A-items and identifying centers of gravity you can better design pilot projects—specific initiatives within the centers of gravity that can be undertaken right away to secure early wins. Implementation plans for pilot projects should define standards to be adhered to, resources needed, and methodology, and should specify both tangible and intangible goals. You should try to both get early wins and establish models of desired behavior that help lay the foundation for deeper change.

Copyright ©2001 by Harvard Business School Publishing. All rights reserved.

THIS PAGE INTENTIONALLY LEFT BLANK

Getting the right kind of wins

The manner in which you achieve tangible results should be consistent with your vision of how the organization ought to work. Careful design and oversight should focus on involving the right people, defining stretch goals, marshaling resources, setting deadlines, pushing for results, and rewarding success. The ultimate goal is a virtuous cycle that reinforces desired behaviors by continually building on modest initial improvements in pursuit of more fundamental changes.

It is also important to achieve your early wins in ways that are *consistent with the culture of your organization*. In some organizational cultures, aggressive individual action is what gets recognized; in others, it's the ability to marshal and lead a team effort. The key is to understand the culture well enough, and early enough, to shape your efforts accordingly.

Use the space below to summarize your current understanding of what your organization values and doesn't value in the pursuit of wins.

_____

_____

_____

_____

_____

_____

_____

_____

_____

_____

_____

_____

Copyright ©2001 by Harvard Business School Publishing. All rights reserved.

THIS PAGE INTENTIONALLY LEFT BLANK

Learning and planning

Learning and planning go hand in hand as you work for early wins. You can't plan if you haven't learned, and you can't learn if you don't plan. You have to do both, but you don't have to learn everything right way. Nor do you have to develop detailed plans for everything right away. You can proceed incrementally, being strategic about prioritizing your learning and developing your plans.

There is a spiral logic to how the process of securing early wins should unfold during the transitional period. As we will see, initial assessments of strategy and performance help you to identify key centers of gravity, which in turn makes possible a deeper assessment of organizational capabilities, and a more focused set of priorities. These priorities equip you to define early pilot projects, whose unfolding teaches you more about the organization, your vision, and so on.

Learning

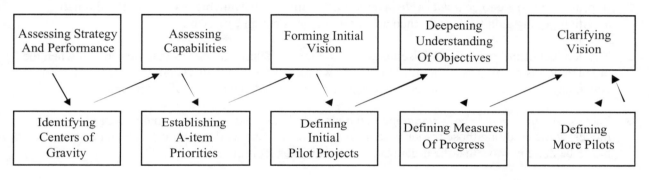

Planning

Identifying centers of gravity

Use the space below to identify no more than two key business processes or problems that present opportunities for getting some early wins.

_____

_____

_____

_____

_____

Copyright ©2001 by Harvard Business School Publishing. All rights reserved.

Criteria for choosing good pilot projects

When setting up pilot projects, you should define the standards to be applied, the resources needed, and the methodology to be employed, and specify both tangible and intangible goals. Promising pilot projects must meet the following criteria to secure early wins:

❑ They must be perceived as *important*. For example, they could target a slow, unpredictable logistics process that has caused tension with customers, or an administrative system that delays approval for needed new equipment.

❑ They must offer opportunities to make *dramatic operational improvements* by attacking persistent problems with new techniques. A slight gain will not be substantial enough to grab people's attention. Also, the improvement must affect operational and financial performance. Merely improving some skills is not good enough.

❑ Improvements have to be *achievable* in a reasonable time with available resources. If a dramatic, attention-getting gain takes more than a few months, it is not an early win.

❑ The conduct of the project should serve as a *model* for the behavioral norms that will prevail when the organization is running as it should. Thus, early wins can illustrate your vision for the organization concretely. They can also allow employees to try out new behaviors in a safe, experimental way.

❑ Success should *enhance your standing.* You must be conspicuous as the essential visionary and prime mover, while crediting those responsible for making the project work. Your effort to get early wins has to be done in ways that the organization recognizes as legitimate.

Now use the space on the next page to plan how you will secure early wins.

Planning to secure early wins

Use the space below to describe the first pilot projects you will initiate. Keep in mind that you can have multiple projects addressing issues in each center of gravity, so long as they are synergistic and you don't get spread too thin. Be as specific as you can about goals, resources, and time-frame for each project.

1. _____

_____

2. _____

_____

3. _____

_____

4. _____

_____

5. _____

_____

6. _____

_____

7. _____

_____

Copyright ©2001 by Harvard Business School Publishing. All rights reserved.

THIS PAGE INTENTIONALLY LEFT BLANK

LAYING A FOUNDATION

Early wins get you off to a good start, but they are not sufficient for continued success. You must also lay a foundation for the changes needed to improve the organization's performance. As mentioned previously, the process resembles the launching of a two-stage rocket; early wins lift you off the ground, and foundation-building provides the thrust to achieve orbit and avoid falling back to earth.

There are limits to how much you can do during your transition to lay the foundation for deeper change. Except in turnarounds, key people will not be let go, strategy will not be changed, major plants will not be closed or relocated, and new products will not be scrapped. Ordinarily, foundation-building during the transition period should focus on *building your team* and on *getting started on cultural change.*

Copyright ©2001 by Harvard Business School Publishing. All rights reserved.

Building your team

Building your team is the most important foundation-building task of your transition. As we have seen, sticking with the existing team too long is a common mistake. By the end of the transition period you must have decided who will stay and who will go; otherwise you will own the team, warts and all. (For high-visibility positions, you must also have plans in place to help the people you replace make their own transitions without delay.)

Focus first on assessing your existing team. Then put on your design hat to think about team composition and team process. (*Composition* refers to who constitutes the team, and *process* refers to how they work together.) Having the right people in the right places isn't enough; they have to be efficient and effective in how they work together.

Assessing your existing team

Rapid, accurate assessments of the existing team are an essential part of your early learning. Unless you are unusually fortunate, you will inherit some good performers, some average performers, and some who aren't up to the job. You will also have to grapple with the politics of the team, including the likelihood that some of its members hoped to get your job. If you come from outside into a realignment or success-sustaining situation, many people will be asking, "Why did he or she get the job?"

Evaluate each member of your existing team on four key criteria:

- ❑ *Competence & judgment.* Do they have the technical competence, experience, and good judgment to do the job effectively?

- ❑ *Energy & focus.* Do they bring the necessary energy and focus to the job, or are they burned-out or unengaged by the challenges you are facing?

- ❑ *Relationships.* Do they get along with others on the team and support team decision making?

- ❑ *Trust & integrity.* Can you fundamentally trust them to do what they say they will do and to support their commitments?

You should strongly consider replacing any existing team member about whom you answer no to any of these questions.

Making early assessments

Review available performance data on members of your team, supplemented by appraisals. If the organization performs climate or morale surveys by unit, these will also provide insight.

Meet members of your new team very early on, and carefully observe them both individually and collectively. Depending on your style preferences, initial meetings with your new subordinates may be informal discussions, more formal reviews of their realms, or a combination. It may make sense to undertake structured interviews of the top team, asking such questions as:

- What do you think of the existing strategy?

- What are the biggest challenges and opportunities we face in the short term? In the long term?

- What resources could we leverage more effectively?

- What changes would you favor in how the team works together?

- If you were me, what would you be paying attention to?

Assessing individuals. Look at what individuals say and at what they don't say. Do they volunteer information or does it have to be pulled out of them bit by bit? Do they take responsibility for problems in their jurisdictions or point fingers? Do they seem knowledgeable, trustworthy, and energetic? Do their relationships with other team members appear cordial and productive? What topics seem to elicit strong emotional responses? (Hot buttons provide important clues about motivation and reservoirs of emotional energy that can block or promote needed change.) Are their expressions and body language consistent with their words?

Evaluating consistency. Also assess the consistency of responses within the team. Are their responses too consistent, indicating an agreed-on "party line"? Or are they so inconsistent as to raise questions about coherence and teamwork? What are the likely implications for your ability to work with the team?

Probing group dynamics. Test your provisional insights and examine relationships and coalitions by observing how the team interacts in early meetings. When one person speaks, others' reactions can say a lot about attitudes, leadership, and alliances. While you listen, pay attention to what is going on among the other listeners. Who seems to defer to whom on a given topic? Do some people roll their eyes or otherwise express disagreement or frustration?

Copyright ©2001 by Harvard Business School Publishing. All rights reserved.

THIS PAGE INTENTIONALLY LEFT BLANK

Making initial judgments

The purpose of your early assessments is to arrive at initial judgments—within a couple of months—about the capabilities and futures of members of your existing team. Specifically, you should assign each team member to one of the following six categories:

- ❑ *Keep in existing position (high-performing)*—currently performing optimally in existing job

- ❑ *Keep in existing position (developmental)*—needs development for which time is available

- ❑ *Keep but move to different position*—strong performer but not in ideal position

- ❑ *On probation*—watch this person carefully and put in place a personal development plan as soon as possible

- ❑ *Don't keep (high priority)*— replace as soon as possible

- ❑ *Don't keep (low priority)*— replace in the medium term

Use the table below to assess your existing team, keeping in mind that these are initial assessments and that you may change your mind.

Individual	Assessment
1.	
2.	
3.	
4.	
5.	
6.	
7.	

Copyright ©2001 by Harvard Business School Publishing. All rights reserved.

THIS PAGE INTENTIONALLY LEFT BLANK

Restructuring your team

Restructuring a management team is like repairing an airplane in mid-flight. It's essential to do the repairs, but you have to be sure not to crash it in the process. Careful balance is necessary between making changes to lay a foundation for superior long-term performance and the need for acceptable short-run results and early wins. If the people who need to be replaced are responsible for parts of the business that can continue running for a while without them, or if replacements can be brought up-to-speed quickly, you should proceed without delay. If not, you may have to defer making your moves until you can find replacements externally or develop them internally.

It also is essential that you have begun to think through your goals, changes in the strategy and the implications for the structure of the organization, the necessary skills, and hence for the composition of the ideal team. It's tough to make good decisions about the team in isolation from other key design decisions. We discussed these in the section on the Design Challenge.

The bottom line is careful thought about the sequencing and timing of moves to restructure your team. Use the space below to identify and prioritize the team-restructuring moves you plan to make in the short term (three months), medium term (three to six months), and long term (six months to a year).

Sequencing your moves

Short-term Priorities	Medium-term priorities	Long-term priorities
1.	1.	1.
2.	2.	2.
3.	3.	3.
4.	4.	4.
5.	5.	5.

Use the space below to identify potential barriers to implementing your plan.

_____

_____

_____

Copyright ©2001 by Harvard Business School Publishing. All rights reserved.

THIS PAGE INTENTIONALLY LEFT BLANK

Avoiding potential pitfalls

The following rules of thumb will help you avoid common traps when restructuring a management team.

Principle 1. Postpone team building until the core is in place.

It's tempting to launch team-building activities such as joint problem-solving, brainstorming, and visioning early on. New leaders, especially those with a consensus-building style, are understandably eager to tap the insights of their top people. There is a danger, though, of deepening the bonds within a group some of whose members are not going to make it. So it's best to avoid explicit team-building activities until the team you want is in place. This doesn't mean that you shouldn't meet as a group. It means that you should put more emphasis on problem solving and decision making one-on-one or with subgroups of the team who are keepers.

Principle 2. Try to defer decisions for which team ownership is essential.

A related mistake is making decisions that should have been deferred until more of your team is in place. Decisions that commit new people to courses of action they had no part in defining are especially undesirable. Of course, you will have to make tough calls early on. But the benefits of moving quickly should be weighed against lost opportunities to solicit insight from new team members and to engender feelings of ownership in them.

Principle 3. Get help with the restructuring process.

The process of replacing people is fraught with legal and company-policy pitfalls. This is not something you should undertake on your own. Find out who can advise you on the process and help you to chart strategy. The support of a good human resources person is invaluable early on.

Principle 4. Move quickly once you have made up your mind.

When you decide that someone must leave, it's important to move quickly and not prolong the inevitable. Explain the situation to the person and explore options with him or her. Then move on.

Principle 5. Strive to preserve the dignity of the people involved.

Personnel changes must be perceived as fair and respectful of the dignity of the individuals involved. Even if other employees agree that a person should be replaced, your credibility will suffer if your actions are perceived as unfair. If you are to be credited with making appropriate personnel choices, you must be seen as making careful assessments of capabilities and fit. Peoples' opinions often hinge on whether you shave sought other options for a well-regarded employee who is ill-suited to a particular job.

Copyright ©2001 by Harvard Business School Publishing. All rights reserved.

THIS PAGE INTENTIONALLY LEFT BLANK

Diagnosing and supporting your new team

You can diagnose the situations facing members of your new team (both keepers and new people) using the basic framework presented in Part One of this workbook in the same way you diagnosed your own situation. Take some time to think about the kind of transition situations each is facing. Even if the organization as a whole is engaged in a realignment, individual members of your team may be confronting turnarounds, startups, or even success-sustaining situations. Their situations have obvious implications for the type of support they will need from you. For new team members, the nature of your support will also depend on whether they are insiders or newcomers to the organization.

For people you plan to keep in their current positions, think about what phase each has reached in his or her own era in the organization. Is he or she still in transition, or further along? Is this a time for any of them to think about initiating a new era of change in their own parts of the organization? If so, how will you encourage them to do so? This is especially important for capable people who have been in their positions for a long time.

Use the table below to do an initial diagnosis of the situations facing members of your new team and the implications for how to support and develop them.

Team member	Existing or new member?	If new, insider or outsider?	If existing, where in era?	Situation (startup, turnaround, realignment, or sustaining success)	Implications for support and development
1.					
2.					
3.					
4.					
5.					
6.					
7.					

Copyright ©2001 by Harvard Business School Publishing. All rights reserved.

THIS PAGE INTENTIONALLY LEFT BLANK

Shaping the team process

Getting the right people into the right positions is essential to long-term success. But you also have to weld them into a high-performing team by putting the right team process in place. Understanding how the team you inherited functioned in the past, and how your style differs from that of your predecessor, is instructive. Key questions include:

- ❑ *Frequency*: How often did the team meet? Was this perceived as too often or not often enough?

- ❑ *Participation*: Who was included in which meetings? Were the right people involved?

- ❑ *Agenda-setting:* How was the decision-making agenda set? Were the right problems addressed?

- ❑ *Scope*: How broad or narrow was the team's involvement in decision making? Was the decision-making process centralized or decentralized?

- ❑ *Roles:* What roles did the various participants play? Who, if anyone, acted as a devil's advocate? Who influenced which decisions?

- ❑ *Style*: How did your predecessor prefer to make decisions? Does this approach differ from your style?

Use the space below to summarize what you have learned about decision making before your arrival. What were its strengths and weaknesses?

Strengths	Weaknesses

Drawing on this assessment, what are your priorities for shaping the way decisions get made?

_____

_____

_____

_____

Copyright ©2001 by Harvard Business School Publishing. All rights reserved.

Establishing the new process

Armed with a solid grasp of how things were in the past and how you want them to be, you are now in a position to initiate your target decision-making process. This initiative is part of a larger effort to get the team to jell and to secure some early wins as a group.

Keep in mind that new teams experience characteristic *stages of development*. In the formative stage, members are cautious and may suppress conflict in the name of unity. Later, conflict may erupt as issues of status, involvement, and expertise get worked out and an equilibrium, functional or not, emerges.

These basic guidelines can help you to shape the team process at the outset:

Guideline 1. Carefully lay the groundwork for early meetings.

Lay out the agenda in advance, and meet with team members one-on-one before your first team meeting. One-on-one post-meeting sessions may also be worthwhile, especially after the first meeting.

Guideline 2. Discuss process expectations and style early on.

In early team meetings, explain your expectations about how the process will work. Be clear about how the new process will differ from the old and why. Be forthright about your decision-making style and your expectations about the roles others will play.

Guideline 3. Walk the talk.

Having laid out process you favor, discipline the team to use it. It is also essential to make your actions conform to your statements of intent, lest you undermine yourself.

Guideline 4. Err on the side of heavy-handedness early on.

Trying to establish a new pattern of behavior is like pushing a rock up one side of a hill and down the other. You have to exert a lot of effort early on to move the rock and keep it moving. But once you get over the hump, momentum will carry it along. Stick to a structured decision-making format early on, until it becomes internalized.

Guideline 5. Demonstrate thoughtful flexibility.

This is the flip side of the previous guideline. You can't afford to approach all problems in the same way. For example, if you believe in building consensus among subordinates, should you always try to do so? With a problem whose solution is likely to create winners and losers, trying to build consensus risks generating a lot of conflict; you would be better off shifting to a consult-and-decide mode. If you consistently approach similar problems in similar ways, this should not create undue confusion.

Understanding the impact of your style

The Assessment of Leadership Style (both your self-assessment and observer assessment) is designed to help you think about the key components of your leadership style. As stressed in the assessment, style is about preferences and inclinations, not abilities. At the same time, differences in style are a key reason for friction between bosses and subordinates and among members of management teams.

"Style" covers a lot of territory and it's essential that you unpack it and look at the key components: learning style, communication style, motivational style, and decision-making style:

❑ Your *learning style* describes your preferences for learning about things. See page 164 to see how you assessed yourself. Are you a hard data or a soft data person? Are you more experiential in your approach to learning about new things or more conceptual?

❑ Your *communication style* describes how you prefer others (for example with subordinates) to communicate with you. See page 164 to see how you assessed yourself. What mode of communication do you prefer? How often do you want communication to occur? What content do you want to see?

❑ Your *motivational style* describes your preferences for being motivated and motivating others. See page 165 to see how you assessed yourself. Do you prefer to motivate others through pull methods or through push methods? How do you prefer to be motivated yourself? To what extent do you adjust your approach to motivation based on who you are dealing with?

❑ Your *decision-making style* describes your preferences for making decisions. See page 166 to see how you assessed yourself. Do you prefer to build consensus or consult with others and make the call? Do you delegate more or less than the "average" manager? To what extent do you adjust your approach to decision making based on the situation?

There are a few classic traps into which you can fall when dealing with people with different styles. One is to interpret style differences as a lack of capability on the part of others. A second, related trap is to deal with others the way you prefer to be dealt with, not adjusting your style to fit the circumstances. A third is to build a team consisting of people whose styles are comfortably similar to your own.

The dangers of doing this are obvious. The first defense is self-awareness. Beyond that you have to be willing to push yourself to adjust when situations demand it. Finally, you should think about building a team consisting of people with different but complementary styles.

Copyright ©2001 by Harvard Business School Publishing. All rights reserved.

THIS PAGE INTENTIONALLY LEFT BLANK

Assessing others' styles

Now take a few minutes to assess your boss and key subordinates on the four dimensions of style. How do their styles match up with yours?

Person	Learning Style	Communication Style	Motivational Style	Decision-making Style
1.				
2.				
3.				
4.				
5.				
6.				
7.				

What are the implications for managing team process? For recruiting new members of your team?

_____

_____

_____

_____

_____

_____

Copyright ©2001 by Harvard Business School Publishing. All rights reserved.

THIS PAGE INTENTIONALLY LEFT BLANK

Getting started on cultural change

It takes a long time to reshape a work culture, but you can and should get the process started during the transition. Whatever the nature of the cultural change you consider necessary, it will call for people to think differently and consider new ways of operating. These basic principles can guide you in effecting cultural change:

Principle 1. Use behavioral change to drive attitude change.

Rather than trying to change peoples' attitudes directly, focus on changing how they behave. Success will gradually change how they think and what they believe.

Principle 2. Align push and pull tools.

Push tools include written strategies, compensation plans, measurement systems, mission statements, strategic plans, annual budgets, and the like. Such tools depend for their effectiveness on authority, loyalty, fear, and the expectation of reward. Pull tools, especially a compelling vision, inspire people by invoking an attractive future. For people to want to change, they must come to believe that new ways of operating will meet their needs better than existing approaches do.

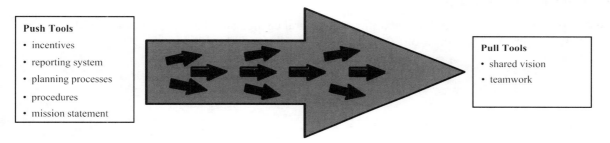

Push Tools
- incentives
- reporting system
- planning processes
- procedures
- mission statement

Pull Tools
- shared vision
- teamwork

Push tools align effort through authority, fear and reward. Pull tools align effort through inspiration. To use pull tools the leader must have very strong visioning and communication skills.

Principle 3. Identify and elevate islands of excellence.

Islands of excellence in your organization may consist of innovative people or groups that haven't been given enough scope, underutilized technologies, or projects that have languished for lack of funding. You can leverage your efforts to change the culture by providing them the resources necessary to have a bigger impact and serve as examples to motivate the rest of the organization.

Principle 4. Build a bridge from the past to the future.

Identify and build on the strengths of the existing culture while you address its weaknesses. An organization can be both proud and complacent. That pride is a resource that you can use to tackle the complacency.

Copyright ©2001 by Harvard Business School Publishing. All rights reserved.

Tools for initiating cultural change

Your earliest steps to begin to change the culture ought to be synergistic with your pursuit of early wins. Five ways to start the process of culture change during your transition are summarized below.

Tool 1. Set up pilot projects: Your pilot projects represent not just early wins for you, but also experiments in which employees can try out new tools and new behavior.

Tool 2. Change the way performance is measured: Change the metrics by which success is judged, and align the objectives of managers and employees with those new metrics.

Tool 3. Educate and involve: Expose people to new ways of operating and thinking about the business, particularly new perspectives on customers and competitors.

Tool 4. Collectively envision new ways to operate: Find ways to bring together people so they can envision a new approach to doing business.

Tool 5. Import someone to stimulate creativity: Import an outside facilitator to stimulate creativity in specific parts of the organization. Choose the outside person with care, lest he or she provoke serious resistance.

Planning for cultural change

Use the space below to identify your priorities for cultural change and the approaches you will use. What strengths will you draw on? What problems will you address?

_____

_____

_____

_____

_____

_____

_____

_____

_____

_____

PART FOUR:
PERSONAL ASSESSMENT INVENTORIES

Overview

Transitioning to a new leadership position is challenging and complex. Effective new leaders use self-diagnosis and reflection to help them effectively deal with the pressures presented during the transition period. Self-diagnosis and reflection help them to gain perspective as well as to establish control over their surroundings.

This three-part assessment inventory will help you to reflect more deeply about your experience in making transitions as well as your style and reactions to stress.

Copyright ©2001 by Harvard Business School Publishing. All rights reserved.

THIS PAGE INTENTIONALLY LEFT BLANK

4A. ASSESSMENT OF TRANSITION EXPERIENCE

This inventory will help you to reflect on and assess your previous experience making transitions to new positions.

Your transition profile

As a starting point, think about all the transitions to new positions you have made *since accepting your first managerial/supervisory position* and answer the following questions:

How many transitions to new management/supervisor positions have you made so far in your career (including the first one)?

_____ transitions

How many years in total have you spent in management/supervisory positions so far?

_____ years

Divide the number of transitions in question 1 by the number of years in question 2 to calculate your average tenure in each position.

_____ average years/position

How many of your transitions to new positions involved:

Moving from one function to another   _____

Moving between business units   _____

Moving between companies   _____

Moving from line to staff or staff to line   _____

Moving to another country   _____

What are the three most difficult types of transitions you have made (for instance, first management position, first general-manager position)? (1 = average difficulty, 5 = extreme difficulty).

a. _____ Difficulty level _____

b. _____ Difficulty level _____

c. _____ Difficulty level _____

Copyright ©2001 by Harvard Business School Publishing. All rights reserved.

Of all the transitions you have experienced so far in your career, which one contributed most to your personal development?

_____

_____

What were the most important things you learned?

_____

_____

Based on your own experience in making transitions and in observing others make transitions, what are the three most common traps into which new leaders fall during their transitions?

Trap # 1. _____

Trap # 2. _____

Trap # 3. _____

Experience with your last transition

Now answer the remaining questions by thinking about your last transition (i.e., not this one if you are currently in transition). Even if your last transition took place several years ago, try to recall what you did and how things went.

Into what position did you last transition (i.e., not the current position if you are presently in transition)?

_____

Overall, how effectively do you think you managed your last transition?

1	2	3	4	5	6	7
Very poorly	Poorly	Somewhat poorly	Neither well nor poorly	Somewhat well	Well	Very well

What didn't go as well as you hoped it would?

_____

_____

Leveraging Your Time Before Entry

How well did you succeed at *leveraging the time you had to prepare* before entering your last new job?

1	2	3	4	5	6	7
Very poorly	Poorly	Somewhat poorly	Neither well nor poorly	Somewhat well	Well	Very well

Are you planning to approach using the time before entry differently this time? If so, how?

_____

_____

Cultural and Political Learning

How well did you succeed at quickl*y learning about the culture and politics* of your new organization last time?

1	2	3	4	5	6	7
Very poorly	Poorly	Somewhat poorly	Neither well nor poorly	Somewhat well	Well	Very well

Are you planning to approach learning about your new organization differently this time? If so, how?

_____

_____

Securing Early Wins

How well did you succeed at *securing early wins* in your new organization during your last transition?

1	2	3	4	5	6	7
Very poorly	Poorly	Somewhat poorly	Neither well nor poorly	Somewhat well	Well	Very well

Are you planning to approach securing early wins differently this time? If so, how?

_____

_____

Copyright ©2001 by Harvard Business School Publishing. All rights reserved.

Laying a Foundation for Fundamental Improvement

How well did you succeed at *laying a foundation for fundamental improvement* in the performance of your new organization during your last transition?

1	2	3	4	5	6	7
Very Poorly	Poorly	Somewhat poorly	Neither well nor poorly	Somewhat well	Well	Very well

Are you planning to approach laying a foundation for improvement differently this time? If so, how?

_____

_____

Creating a Personal Vision

How well did you succeed at *creating a personal vision* for what new organization should become during your last transition?

1	2	3	4	5	6	7
Very Poorly	Poorly	Somewhat poorly	Neither well nor poorly	Somewhat well	Well	Very well

Are you planning to approach creating a vision differently this time? If so, how?

_____

_____

Developing a Relationship with Your New Boss

How well did you succeed at *developing a productive relationship with your new boss* during your last transition?

1	2	3	4	5	6	7
Very Poorly	Poorly	Somewhat poorly	Neither well nor poorly	Somewhat well	Well	Very well

Are you planning to approach developing a relationship with your new boss differently this time? If so, how?

_____

_____

Building Your Team

How well did you succeed at *building the right team* for your new organization last time?

1	2	3	4	5	6	7
Very Poorly	Poorly	Somewhat poorly	Neither well nor poorly	Somewhat well	Well	Very well

Are you planning to approach building your team differently this time? If so, how?

_____

_____

External Coalition Building

How well did you succeed at *building supportive coalitions outside your organization* last time?

1	2	3	4	5	6	7
Very Poorly	Poorly	Somewhat poorly	Neither well nor poorly	Somewhat well	Well	Very well

Are you planning to approach building coalitions differently this time? If so, how?

_____

_____

Maintaining Balance and Self-awareness

How well did you succeed at *maintaining balance and self-awareness* during your last transition?

1	2	3	4	5	6	7
Very Poorly	Poorly	Somewhat poorly	Neither well nor poorly	Somewhat well	Well	Very well

Are you planning to maintaining balance and self-awareness differently this time? If so, how?

_____

_____

Copyright ©2001 by Harvard Business School Publishing. All rights reserved.

THIS PAGE INTENTIONALLY LEFT BLANK

4B. ASSESSMENT OF LEADERSHIP STYLE

This assessment will help you assess your leadership style and how it may be helping or hindering you. Style is a matter of preferences and inclinations, not abilities. It has to do with what you prefer to do and how you prefer to act in particular situations. Style runs deep, but it isn't destiny.

Assessing your problem preferences

Every leader prefers certain kinds of problems and challenges. This is not a matter of avoiding certain problems; it is a question of *preferences*. The table that follows is a simple tool for assessing your preferences.

For each cell in the table, assess your intrinsic interest in *solving problems* in the domain in question. In the first row, for example, ask yourself how much you like to redesign appraisal-and-reward systems, how much you like to deal with employee morale issues, and how much you like to grapple with matters of equity and fairness.

Rank each item separately, on a scale of 1 (not at all) to 10 (very much). *Keep in mind that you are being asked about your intrinsic interest in problems of different kinds, not your skill or experience.*

appraisal-and-reward system design	employee morale	equity/fairness
_____	_____	_____
management of financial risk	budgeting	cost-consciousness
		_____
product positioning	relationships with customers	customer focus
_____	_____	_____
product or service quality	relationships with distributors and suppliers	continuous improvement
_____	_____	_____
project-management systems	relationships among R&D, Marketing, and Operations	cross-functional cooperation
_____	_____	_____

**DO NOT TURN THE PAGE BEFORE
COMPLETING THE TABLE**

Copyright ©2001 by Harvard Business School Publishing. All rights reserved.

Transfer your scores from the table on the previous page to the corresponding cells in the table below, and sum the three vertical columns. These column totals represent your preferences among technical, cultural, and political problems. If one number is substantially lower than the rest, it represents a potential blind spot.

Then sum the totals for the five horizontal rows. These totals represent your preferences among function-related problems.

Function	Technical	Political	Cultural	Total
Human Resources				_____
Finance				_____
Marketing				_____
Operations				_____
Research and Development				_____
Total	_____	_____	_____	_____

In what spheres are you most and least interested in solving problems? Why?

_____

_____

What are the implications of your problem preferences for potential blind spots during a transition?

_____

_____

Assessing Your Leadership Style

Differences between my leadership style and those of others have proven to be problematic in previous positions.

1	2	3	4	5	6	7
Strongly disagree	Disagree	Somewhat disagree	Neither agree nor disagree	Somewhat agree	Agree	Strongly agree

What was the most difficult situation involving style differences that you have faced in the past and how did you deal with it?

_____

_____

_____

"Style" encompasses a wide array of leadership behaviors. So it's useful to unbundle the elements of leadership style in order to better understand how you and others behave. In this instrument, four distinct elements of leadership style are assessed:

❑ *Learning style* – how you prefer to learn

❑ *Communication style* – how you prefer to communicate with others

❑ *Motivational style* – how you prefer to motivate others and be motivated

❑ *Decision-making style* – how you prefer to make important decisions

Copyright ©2001 by Harvard Business School Publishing. All rights reserved.

Learning Style

This section will help you assess how you prefer to *learn*.

On balance, do you put more stock in hard data (numbers and analyses) or soft data (expert assessments and others' observations)? **Note:** You probably rely on both, but which do you give more credence to?

❑ Hard data ❑ Soft data

On balance, do you prefer to learn by diving into a situation (an experiential learning style) or by observing for a while before taking action (a conceptual learning style)? **Note:** Once again, you probably do both, but which feels most natural to you?

❑ Dive in ❑ Observe for a while

What are the implications of your learning style for potential blind spots during a transition?

_____

_____

_____

_____

Communication Style

This section will help you assess how you prefer to *communicate with others*.

On balance, do you like subordinates to communicate with you in writing (including e-mail) or in conversation (including voicemail)?

❑ Writing ❑ Conversation

On balance, how often do you prefer to interact with key subordinates in a given week? _____times

What are the implications of your communication style for potential blind spots during a transition?

_____

_____

_____

Motivational Style

This section will help you assess how you prefer to *motivate others and to be motivated yourself.*

Do you tend to motivate people more through "push" methods, such as setting goals, measuring performance, and defining rewards and punishments, or "pull" methods such as creating a vision and inspiring teamwork? If you use both methods, identify which you rely on more heavily.

      ❑ Push methods   ❑ Pull methods

Which motivational methods are you yourself more responsive to, push methods or pull methods?

      ❑ Push methods   ❑ Pull methods

To what extent do you change your motivational approach in light of your assessment of how particular individuals prefer to be motivated?

1	2	3	4	5	6	7
Not at all			Occasionally			To a large extent

What are the implications of your motivational style for potential blind spots during a transition?

_____

_____

_____

_____

_____

_____

Copyright ©2001 by Harvard Business School Publishing. All rights reserved.

Decision-making Style

This section will help you assess how you prefer to *make important decisions.*

When you have an important decision to make, do you prefer to (1) consult subordinates and then make the call or to (2) build consensus among your subordinates? If you use both approaches, which do you tend to rely on more?

❑ Consult and then decide   ❑ Build consensus

Do you sometimes change your approach to decision making depending on the issue at hand?

1	2	3	4	5	6	7
Never	Rarely		Occasionally		Often	Very often

In comparison to the typical manager at your level in your organization, do you tend to delegate more or less responsibility to subordinates?

❑ Delegate more than average   ❑ Delegate less than average

What are the implications of your decision-making style for potential blind spots during a transition?

_____

_____

_____

_____

_____

4C. Assessment of Reactions to Stress

This assessment will help you gauge your reactions to stress. Transitions are invariably times of pressure and dislocation, when your characteristic responses to stress are likely to be activated. Some may be productive, but others may undermine your capacity to maintain balance and exercise sound judgment. Forewarned is forearmed.

As you complete the assessment, think about periods in the past when you have experienced extreme personal or professional stress. What were your characteristic reactions in such situations?

When I am under great stress, I...

	Strongly Disagree	Disagree	Neither Agree nor Disagree	Agree	Strongly Agree
1. Have more difficulty sleeping.	1	2	3	4	5
2. Feel sharper mentally.	1	2	3	4	5
3. Become more domineering.	1	2	3	4	5
4. Suffer more aches and pains.	1	2	3	4	5
5. Pay more attention to personal relationships.	1	2	3	4	5
6. Become more forgetful.	1	2	3	4	5
7. Feel more isolated.	1	2	3	4	5
8. Feel very focused.	1	2	3	4	5
9. Eat more than usual.	1	2	3	4	5
10. Feel paralyzed by indecision.	1	2	3	4	5
11. Become more judgmental.	1	2	3	4	5
12. Pay less attention to personal grooming.	1	2	3	4	5
13. Feel more energized.	1	2	3	4	5
14. Act more impulsively.	1	2	3	4	5
15. Get "down" more easily.	1	2	3	4	5
16. Exercise more frequently.	1	2	3	4	5
17. Become more patient with others.	1	2	3	4	5
18. Have more difficulty concentrating.	1	2	3	4	5
19. Turn to friends for support.	1	2	3	4	5
20. Feel more anxious.	1	2	3	4	5
21. Get tired more easily.	1	2	3	4	5
22. Drink more than usual.	1	2	3	4	5

DO NOT TURN THE PAGE BEFORE COMPLETING THE TABLE

Copyright ©2001 by Harvard Business School Publishing. All rights reserved.

THIS PAGE INTENTIONALLY LEFT BLANK

Assessing Your Physical, Cognitive, and Emotional Reactions

Now you should process the results from this assessment as follows. The instrument is designed to give you scores on three stress-related indexes:

- ❑ *Physical* – the impact of stress on your physical well-being.
- ❑ *Cognitive* – the impact of stress on your ability to think.
- ❑ *Emotional* – the impact of stress on your emotional state.

Follow the instructions below to calculate your three scores.

	How to Calculate	Your Score
Physical	Add your scores for questions #1, #4, #12, and #21, then subtract your score for question #13, then add 6 and divide the result by 5.	
Cognitive	Add your scores for questions #6, #11, #14, and #18, then subtract your scores for questions #2 and #8, then add 12 and divide the result by 6.	
Emotional	Add your scores for questions #3, #7, #10, #15, and #20, then subtract your score for question #17, then add 6 and divide the result by 6.	
Overall Impact	Add your scores for physical, cognitive, and emotional as calculated above and divide by 3.	

Now take a look at these scores. Lower scores are better. In which of these three areas are you most affected by stress? Is the overall impact of stress on you 2.5 or greater?

Assessing Your Coping Behaviors

The instrument also gives you a score for your *coping behaviors*: the things you do to release or deal with stress. Follow the instructions below to calculate your score for coping behaviors:

Coping Behaviors	Add your scores for questions #9 and #22, then subtract your scores for questions #5, #16, and #19, then add 18 and divide the result by 5.	

Once again, a lower score is better.

Copyright ©2001 by Harvard Business School Publishing. All rights reserved.

To what extent are your reactions to stress visible to people at work?

1	2	3	4	5
Not at all	A little	Somewhat	Quite a bit	To a great extent

To what extent are your reactions to stress visible to members of your immediate family?

1	2	3	4	5
Not at all	A little	Somewhat	Quite a bit	To a great extent

What can you do to cope better with stress during your transition?

_____

_____

_____

_____

_____

_____

PART FIVE: OBSERVER ASSESSMENT FORMS

Overview

The two assessment inventories that follow are for you to copy and give to others to fill out. The first, the Assessment of Transition Experience instrument, inquires about your susceptibility to common traps, approaches to building credibility, and leadership style. The second, the Assessment of Reactions to Stress instrument, looks at your characteristic reactions in situations of stress. Others' observations will give you an external perspective to compare to your own assessments.

Instructions

Identify people you trust and ask them to fill out the forms. Give the Assessment of Transition Experience to approximately three or four people with whom you have worked. Give the Assessment of Reactions to Stress to a mix of family members, friends, and professional associates, ideally one or two of each. Try to find both male and female respondents for both assessments.

Be sure to fill our your own assessments before you look at others' assessments of you. Then compare your assessments with others' assessments. If there are significant differences, why is that the case?

Copyright ©2001 by Harvard Business School Publishing. All rights reserved.

THIS PAGE INTENTIONALLY LEFT BLANK

5A. OBSERVER ASSESSMENT OF TRANSITION EXPERIENCE

The person named below is transitioning into a new leadership role and has asked you to fill out this assessment. Please think about what you know of this person's strengths and weaknesses. Then take a few minutes to answer the following questions. When a question offers two distinct choices, both of which are to some extent true, choose the answer that best describes this person's dominant tendency.

Assessment for _____

Are you a family member, friend, or professional associate of this person? _____

Potential Traps

How susceptible is this person to each of the following common traps into which new leaders fall? Rate them each separately.

Trap	Description	Susceptibility
Falling behind the learning curve	Spending too much time before taking the new job wrapping up current responsibilities or relaxing and not preparing enough.	1----------2----------3----------4----------5 low high
Becoming isolated	Not spending enough time early on talking to employees and other key constituencies.	1----------2----------3----------4----------5 low high
Coming in with the answer	Making up his or her mind prematurely about the problem and the solution.	1----------2----------3----------4----------5 low high
Staying with the existing team too long	Retaining subordinates with a record of mediocre performance in the hope of turning them around.	1----------2----------3----------4----------5 low high
Attempting to do too much	Rushing off in all directions, pushing multiple initiatives in the belief that some will pay off.	1----------2----------3----------4----------5 low high
Allowing capture by the wrong people	Appearing to listen to some people and not others.	1----------2----------3----------4----------5 low high
Setting unrealistic expectations	Failing to negotiate the initial mandate or to establish clear, achievable objectives.	1----------2----------3----------4----------5 low high

Copyright ©2001 by Harvard Business School Publishing. All rights reserved.

Focus on the trap to which you assigned the highest ranking. What is it about this person's style or experience that makes him/her particularly susceptible to this trap?

_____

_____

_____

_____

Building personal credibility

How effective is this person at building personal credibility? Do a separate assessment of each of the credibility drivers listed below.

Credibility driver	Assessment of Effectiveness
Demanding but able to be satisfied	1----------2----------3----------4----------5 low high
Accessible but not too familiar	1----------2----------3----------4----------5 low high
Decisive but judicious	1----------2----------3----------4----------5 low high
Focused but flexible	1----------2----------3----------4----------5 low high
Active without causing commotion	1----------2----------3----------4----------5 low high
Willing to make tough calls but humane	1----------2----------3----------4----------5 low high

Use the space below if you want to comment further.

_____

_____

_____

_____

Leadership Style

How does this person prefer to lead others? Do a separate assessment for each of the elements of leadership style listed below.

Learning Style

On balance, does this person put more stock in hard data (numbers and analyses) or soft data (expert assessments and others' opinions)?

❑ Hard data   ❑ Soft data

On balance, does this person prefer to learn by diving into a situation (an experiential learning style) or by observing for a while before taking action (a conceptual learning style)?

❑ Dive in   ❑ Observe for a while

Communication Style

On balance, does this person prefer that subordinates communicate in writing (including e-mail) or in conversation (including voicemail)?

❑ Writing   ❑ Conversation

Motivational Style

On balance, does this person tend to favor "push" methods of motivating others, such as setting goals, measuring performance, and offering incentives, or "pull" methods like creating a vision and inspiring teamwork?

❑ Push methods   ❑ Pull methods

On balance, does this person respond more to push methods or pull methods?

❑ Push methods   ❑ Pull methods

To what extent does this person change motivational approaches in response to how the people in question prefer to be motivated?

1	2	3	4	5	6	7
Not at all			Occasionally			To a large extent

Copyright ©2001 by Harvard Business School Publishing. All rights reserved.

Decision-making Style

On balance, does this person prefer to make important decisions by (1) consulting with subordinates and then making the call or (2) building consensus among subordinates?

❑ Consult and then decide   ❑ Build consensus

To what extent does this person change decision-making approaches depending on the issues at hand?

1	2	3	4	5	6	7
Not at all	Rarely		Neutral		Often	Very often

In comparison to the typical manager at the same level, does this person tend to delegate more or less responsibility to subordinates?

❑ Delegates more   ❑ Delegates less

Use the space below if you want to comment further.

_____

_____

_____

_____

_____

_____

_____

5B. OBSERVER ASSESSMENT OF REACTIONS TO STRESS

The person named below is transitioning into a new leadership role and has asked you to fill out this assessment. Please think about what you know of this person's strengths and weaknesses.

Assessment for _____

Are you a family member, friend, or professional associate of this person? _____

When this person is under great stress, he or she...

	Strongly Disagree	Disagree	Neither Agree nor Disagree	Agree	Strongly Agree
1. Has more difficulty sleeping.	1	2	3	4	5
2. Seems sharper mentally.	1	2	3	4	5
3. Becomes more domineering.	1	2	3	4	5
4. Suffers more aches and pains.	1	2	3	4	5
5. Pays more attention to personal relationships.	1	2	3	4	5
6. Becomes more forgetful.	1	2	3	4	5
7. Seems more isolated.	1	2	3	4	5
8. Seems more focused.	1	2	3	4	5
9. Eats more than usual.	1	2	3	4	5
10. Gets paralyzed by indecision.	1	2	3	4	5
11. Becomes more judgmental.	1	2	3	4	5
12. Pays less attention to personal grooming.	1	2	3	4	5
13. Seems more energized.	1	2	3	4	5
14. Acts more impulsively.	1	2	3	4	5
15. Gets "down" more easily.	1	2	3	4	5
16. Exercises more frequently.	1	2	3	4	5
17. Becomes more patient with others.	1	2	3	4	5
18. Has more difficulty concentrating.	1	2	3	4	5
19. Turns to friends for support.	1	2	3	4	5
20. Seems more anxious.	1	2	3	4	5
21. Gets tired more easily.	1	2	3	4	5
22. Drinks more than usual.	1	2	3	4	5

Copyright ©2001 by Harvard Business School Publishing. All rights reserved.

THIS PAGE INTENTIONALLY LEFT BLANK

To what extent are this person's reactions to stress visible to people at his or her place of work?

1	2	3	4	5
Not at all	A little	Somewhat	Quite a bit	To a great extent

To what extent are this person's reactions to stress visible to members of his or her immediate family?

1	2	3	4	5
Not at all	A little	Somewhat	Quite a bit	To a great extent

Use the space below if you want to comment further.

_____

_____

_____

_____

_____

_____

_____

Copyright ©2001 by Harvard Business School Publishing. All rights reserved.

THIS PAGE INTENTIONALLY LEFT BLANK

PART SIX: GUIDELINES

This part contains some optional resources that you may draw upon during your transition. These include:

A. Guidelines for establishing learning goals
B. Guidelines for structured reflection

Copyright ©2001 by Harvard Business School Publishing. All rights reserved.

THIS PAGE INTENTIONALLY LEFT BLANK

6A. GUIDELINES FOR ESTABLISHING LEARNING GOALS

The following guidelines will help you figure out what you need to learn during your transition. Specific goals are outlined for learning

❏ prior to entry

❏ by the end of your first week on the job

❏ by the end of your first month on the job

❏ by the end of your first three months on the job

Keep in mind that these questions are just suggestive prompts, not specifications. Your specific priorities will depend on the situation you are facing.

Copyright ©2001 by Harvard Business School Publishing. All rights reserved.

Learning Prior to Entry

Overarching objectives:

- ❏ To develop working hypotheses about the big strategic, technical, and political challenges facing the organization.

- ❏ To finalize a plan for joining the organization.

Key questions:

- ❏ How well do the organization's challenges match my strengths and shortcomings?

- ❏ What signals do I want to send early on?

- ❏ Who should I talk to, and how, to get the simplest and truest read on the organization's strategy and capabilities?

Learning about strategy	Learning about technical capabilities, culture, and politics
❏ What logical gaps are evident in the strategy?	❏ What do outside observers think about how the organization is managed?
❏ What do outside experts believe to be the strengths and weaknesses of the strategy?	❏ What do operating reports reveal about how the organization really runs?
❏ What do the detailed financials say about the organization's real priorities?	❏ What do former employees have to say about the organization?
❏ According to key documents, what does the organization know and not know about its competitors? About its customers?	❏ How effective are the key cross-functional decision-making processes?
❏ Does the sum of the departmental goals and plans match the strategic plan? (For instance, do market-share and growth objectives match new-product plans?)	❏ What evidence is there that top management understands what is happening on the front lines?

Learning by the end of your first week

Overarching objectives:

- ❑ To get off to a good start and figure out where to look more deeply.
- ❑ To begin to test hypotheses about how the organization actually works.

Key questions:

- ❑ How does this place feel to me?
- ❑ What are my initial impressions of the top management team?

Learning about strategy	Learning about technical capabilities, culture, and politics
❑ What does senior management believe to be the organization's main short-term problems and opportunities?	❑ Are people open about the problems they face?
❑ Is there consistency in senior management's assessments?	❑ How much cooperation or conflict does there seem to be among key groups?
❑ What does senior management believe to be the longer-term strategic priorities?	❑ Does the pace of the place match the urgency of solving short-term problems and/or realizing longer-term growth potential?
❑ How much growth potential does senior management see in the organization?	
❑ Are barriers to growth apparent to senior management?	

Copyright ©2001 by Harvard Business School Publishing. All rights reserved.

Learning by the end of your first month

Overarching objectives:

- ❏ To generate working hypotheses about the capabilities of the top-management team.
- ❏ To assess how the organization interacts with customers.
- ❏ To get an initial feel for the organization's technical capabilities.
- ❏ To begin to identify key power coalitions.

Key questions:

- ❏ Where are key opportunities for growth evident?
- ❏ What are the biggest threats we face?
- ❏ Are the right people in the right positions?
- ❏ Do we have the capacity to meet customers' expectations?

Learning about strategy	Learning about technical capabilities, culture, and politics
❏ Does an orientation to customers prevail among top managers?	❏ Do people follow through on what they promise? Do they worry when deadlines are missed?
❏ How do customers rank our service, cost, and quality versus that of our competitors?	❏ Who seems to defer to whom? Who seems to exercise power and why?
❏ Do managers think seriously and substantively about the competition?	❏ Can we deliver what our customers need? Do we have the right operations, sales, and service capabilities?
	❏ Have I heard people praise or criticize the level of skills and knowledge here?
	❏ Do the new products in the pipeline look promising?
	❏ How do the key intra- and cross-functional decision-making processes work?

Learning by the end of your first three months

Overarching objectives:

- ❑ To understand who has power and how decisions get made.
- ❑ To rough out a strategy and capability-building plan for the next 18-36 months.
- ❑ To decide who stays and who goes.
- ❑ To rough out an image of the sort of place this has to become.

Key questions:

- ❑ Which power coalitions are pivotal for the changes I need to make?
- ❑ What must be my A-item priorities?
- ❑ Who has be replaced and how am I going to do it?
- ❑ Whose political support can I count on for what I decide to do?

Learning about strategy	Learning about technical capabilities, culture, and politics
❑ What are our best competitors up to? Why?	❑ Does top management seem to work as a team? Who are the team players?
❑ What are the conceptual flaws in the organization's strategy? How serious are they?	❑ Does a customer orientation prevail throughout the organization?
❑ What do front-line employees think of our service, cost, and quality versus that of our competitors?	❑ Is the talent in place at the top to get the job done? Who is fired up and who isn't?
❑ What do our distributors think of our service, cost, and quality versus that of our competitors?	❑ Will I get the support I need if I move to replace top people?
	❑ What must happen to improve the effectiveness and timeliness of important decisions?
❑ What do our suppliers think of us as customers? Are our suppliers the best choices for us?	❑ How motivated are the people on the front line? Do they get the support they need?

Copyright ©2001 by Harvard Business School Publishing. All rights reserved.

THIS PAGE INTENTIONALLY LEFT BLANK

6B. GUIDELINES FOR STRUCTURED REFLECTION

Make multiple copies of this assessment template. Use it periodically (ideally once a week) to assess how you are doing.

Date: _____

Overall assessment

How do you feel about your current performance in your organization?

1	2	3	4	5	6	7
Extremely dissatisfied	Very dissatisfied	Somewhat dissatisfied	Neutral	Somewhat satisfied	Very satisfied	Extremely satisfied

Detailed assessment: Goals

Use the following questions to evaluate how well you are meeting your goals. Summarize your responses beneath each set of questions.

What do you feel so far?

❑ Do you feel excited? If not, why not? What have you done to block feeling excited? Do you feel confident? If not, why not? What is preventing you from feeling confident?

❑ Do you feel in control of your success? If not, what must you do to gain more control?

_____

_____

_____

What has bothered you so far?

❑ With whom have you not gotten along? Why? What have you done to cause strain?

❑ Of the meetings you have attended, which has been most troubling? Why?

❑ Of all that you have you seen or heard, what has disturbed you most?

_____

_____

_____

Copyright ©2001 by Harvard Business School Publishing. All rights reserved.

What has gone well and poorly?

❑ Of the interactions you've had, which would you handle differently if you had the chance? Which exceeded your expectations? Why?

❑ What decisions have you made that turned out particularly well? Not so well? Why?

❑ Of the opportunities you've missed, was a better result blocked primarily by you or by something beyond your control?

_____

_____

_____

Meeting the four challenges

Use the following questions to evaluate how well you are meeting the four challenges. Summarize your responses beneath each set of questions.

Learning: How is your learning going? Is the balance right among technical, cultural, and political learning? What are your priorities for learning?

_____

_____

_____

Influence: How are you doing at influencing key groups, internally and externally? What coalitions do you most need to build?

_____

_____

_____

Design: What progress have you made in assessing the existing strategy and altering it if necessary? In aligning strategy, structure, systems, and skills? What are your priorities?

_____

_____

_____

Self-management: Have style issues been a problem so far? If so, what can you do about it? Are you using advice and counsel effectively? What are your priorities for building your advice-and-counsel network?

_____

_____

_____

In light of this self-assessment, what are you going to do differently?

_____

_____

_____

_____

_____

_____

_____

_____

_____

_____

_____

_____

Copyright ©2001 by Harvard Business School Publishing. All rights reserved.